MULTIFARIOUS FUNK
THE EVOLUTION AND BIOGRAPHY OF
GEORGE CLINTON
AND THE PARLIAMENT-FUNKADELIC EMPIRE

**(FUNKENTELECHY)
HOW'S YOUR FUNK!**

MULTIFARIOUS FUNK
THE EVOLUTION AND BIOGRAPHY OF
GEORGE CLINTON
AND THE PARLIAMENT-FUNKADELIC EMPIRE

(FUNKENTELECHY)
HOW'S YOUR FUNK!

Written by SABRINA-MARIE
Edited by TONY ROSE

RETRO BOOKS
PHOENIX / NEW YORK / LOS ANGELES
WWW.AMBERBOOKS.COM
WWW.TONYROSEENTERPRISES.COM

MULTIFARIOUS FUNK
THE EVOLUTION AND BIOGRAPHY OF
GEORGE CLINTON
And the Parliament-Funkadelic Empire

Retro Books is an imprint of Colossus Books
A Division of Amber Communications Group, Inc.
1334 East Chandler Boulevard, Suite 5-D67
Phoenix, AZ 85048
Amberbk@aol.com
WWW.AMBERBOOKS.COM
WWW.TONYROSEENTERPRISES.COM

Tony Rose, Publisher/Editorial Director
Yvonne Rose, Associate Publisher
The Printed Page, Interior Design / Cover Layout

"Multifarious Funk" Edited with Additional Writing by Tony Rose

All rights reserved. No part of this book may be used, reproduced or transmitted in any form or by any means—electronic or mechanical, including photocopying, recording or by any information storage and retrieved system without written permission from the publisher, except for the inclusion of brief quotations in a review or critical article.

RETRO BOOKS are available at special discounts for bulk purchases, sales promotions, fund raising or educational purposes.

Copyright © 2017 by Amber Books and Sabrina-Marie Wilson
ISBN #: 978-1-937269-65-4
Ebook ISBN #: 978-1-937269-66-1

Library of Congress Cataloging-in-Publication Data

Names: Wilson, Sabrina-Marie author. | Rose, Tony, 1953-
Title: Multifarious funk - the evolution and biography of George Clinton and the Parliament-Funkadelic empire : (funkentelechy) how's your funk! / written by Sabrina-Marie; edited by Tony Rose.
Description: Phoenix, AZ : Retro Books, [2017] | Includes bibliographical references.
Identifiers: LCCN 2017018812 | ISBN 9781937269654 (pbk.)
Subjects: LCSH: Clinton, George, 1940- | Funk musicians--United States--Biography. | Funkadelic (Musical group) | Parliament (Musical group)
Classification: LCC ML420.C575 W5 2015 | DDC 782.421644092 [B] --dc23
LC record available at https://lccn.loc.gov/2017018812

CONTENTS

About the Author	ix
Introduction	1
1. Funky Beginnings	5
2. Bootcamp and Entertainment Realities	19
3. Fatherhood & Work Gigs	23
4. Labels and Liaisons	27
5. Lasting Connections and Transforming Genres	35
6. Canceled By 2 Riots, Parliaments Undaunted	39
7. Age of Hippie Change	43
8. Loads of Musical Potpourri	45
9. Detroit's Shock Rock	49
10. Merging Adelic With Funk. The Beginning	53
11. Eclectic Imaging	63
12. Charting Fresh Territory	71
13. 60's 70's Space, Cosmic Influence and George	75
14. Original P Checked Out	81
15. Takin' It to the Mothership	85
16. Agents of Supergroovalisticprosifunkstication	91
17. R&B, Crossover vs. Real Funk	95
18. UnDisco Niche	99
19. Casablanca Records Sky High Blow.............	103
20. P-Funkology 101	107
21. The Dr. Of Funk	109
22. Funkology Movement	113
23. Mega Tribe Support	117
24. It's B Bootsy Baby Baba	119
25. The Funkadelica Thang	127
26. Expanding the Funk Empire	129
27. Uncle Jam Records-distributed	137

28. What is Funkin' Soul? 153
29. Purple Reign 157
30. A Parliafunkadelicment Thang 159
31. Evolving Funk 161
32. United Sound Systems Recording Studios 165
33. George Clinton 167
References 171

ABOUT THE AUTHOR

Sabrina-Marie

In exploring funk icon *George Clinton*, I had a lot of fun researching and writing about his early introductions to blues, jazz, doo wop, and R&B music, says *Sabrina-Marie*, author of the book **Mutifarious Funk"**. Over many decades, George traveled through a unique university of musicology that included singers, songwriters, musicians, record moguls, and marketing geniuses. He networked and worked with everyone from rock and roll upstarts, music icons, soul legends and folk artists, early in his career."

Later on George would cultivate alliances with young music prodigies like the late *Dr. Bernie Worrell, Bill Nelson, Jerome Brailey, Bootsy & Catfish Collins, Garry Shider, Glen Goins,* and many other multi-talented musicians and vocalists. This collaboration helped to expand George's career with *Parliament-Funkadelic* and imprint his influence on music artists and rappers for several generations. I hope that you will enjoy reading about George Clinton's life as much as I enjoyed writing about it. - Sabrina-Marie

Sabrina-Marie enjoys studying music history and pop culture. She is a proud East Coast native and enjoys traveling. In addition, she is a vegetarian, devoted to naturopathic health and wellness, green energy and a fashionista in progress. She also writes articles for national beauty, health and fitness publications.

Introduction
FROM THE PUBLISHER

Tony Rose, "retro" 1970s

While editing and preparing for publication this brilliant book by Sabrina-Marie on the extraordinary life of the living musical genius that is **George Clinton,** founder of the **Parliament-Funkadelic empire**, I began to remember and realize that I had once been a weed smoking, drug taking, alcohol drinking, no head, no backstage pass, full-fledged, dues paying, card carrying member of the **Parliament-Funkadelic Nation,** a true funkateer. My motherfunkin ass had danced and gotten high many times while partying and jammin' to the music of **The Parliaments**, then the **Funkadelics**, and then **Parliament-Funkadelics**, through the late 60's, all through the 70's, and I felt that I was always, truly, standing on the verge of gettin' it on and doing something great.

Multifarious Funk

I had funkafied hundreds and hundreds and hundreds, if not thousands of girls while living in Boston, then Japan, South Korea, South Vietnam and even some North Vietnamese girls, then some Northern California girls, then back to Boston girls, then some cross country American ghetto girls, then some Los Angeles girls and then some Chicago girls, then funkafied some more back in Boston girls, to the music of the **Funkadelic albums**, *Free Your Mind... and Your Ass Will Follow, Maggot Brain, America Eats Its Young, Cosmic Slop, Standing on the Verge of Getting It On, Let's Take It to the Stage, Tales of Kidd Funkadelic, Hardcore Jollies, One Nation Under a Groove, Uncle Jam Wants You.*

And the, **Funkadelic singles**, *Music for My Mother, I'll Bet You, I Got a Thing, You Got a Thing, Everybody's Got a Thing, I Wanna Know If It's Good to You?, You and Your Folks, Me and My Folks, Can You Get to That, Hit It and Quit It, A Joyful Process, Loose Booty, Cosmic Slop, Standing on the Verge of Getting It On, Red Hot Momma, Get Off Your Ass and Jam, Better by the Pound, Let's Take It to the Stage, Undisco Kidd, Comin' Round the Mountain, Smokey, One Nation Under a Groove, Cholly (Funk Getting Ready To Roll!), (Not Just) Knee Deep, Uncle Jam.*

And then the, **Parliament albums**, *Up for the Down Stroke, Chocolate City, Mothership Connection, The Clones of Dr. Funkenstein, Funkentelechy Vs. the Placebo Syndrome, Motor Booty Affair, Gloryhallastoopid, Trombipulation,* and the infamous, **Parliament singles**, *Breakdown, Up For The Down Stroke, Testify, Chocolate City, Ride On, Chocolate City, P. Funk (Wants to Get Funked Up), Tear The Roof Off The Sucker (Give Up The Funk), Mothership Connection (Star Child), Do That Stuff, Dr. Funkenstein, Fantasy Is Reality, Bop Gun (Endangered Species), Flash Light, Funkentelechy, Aqua Boogie (A Psychoalphadiscobetabioaquadoloop, Rumpofsteelskin, Party People, Theme From The Black Hole, The Big Bang Theory, Agony of DeFeet,* with *Funkentelechy* being my favorite song of all time to funk the girls and the world with, to sing to, write to, and play to.

And by the time it's early 1979 and I meet **Maurice Starr**, and his song *About Time I Funk You Baby*, I was ready to free my mind and let my ass follow, and then I would meet, manage and produce, **Prince Charles Alexander** and do a song called *In the Streets*, by *Prince Charles and the City Beat Band*, and we absolutely and magnificently, truly, funkafied the whole world, all thanks to the master, the legend, the master blaster of all that is funky, the Bop Gun himself, **George Clinton**, who made us and hundreds of his second and third generation funkateers, not just knee deep in the funk, but one nation under the groove! So, I dedicate this first **Retro Book** on the life of **George Clinton**, to my old back in the day musician friends, **Prince Charles Alexander and Maurice Starr,** two of the funkiest cats ever.

—**Tony Rose**

Tony Rose is an NAACP Image Award Winner for Outstanding Literature and the Publisher and CEO of Phoenix, AZ based, Amber Communications Group, Inc., the nation's largest African-American Publisher of Self-Help Books and Music Biographies.

He was born in Roxbury (Boston) Massachusetts and raised in the Whittier Street Housing Projects. He was honorably discharged from the U.S. Air Force after serving in the Vietnam War, and attended the University of Massachusetts, the University of California in Los Angeles and the New England Conservatory of Music, Boston, MA. He was employed as a production assistant at the Burbank Studios (Warner Brothers and Columbia Pictures), in the accounting and sales division at Warner/Electra/Atlantic Records (WEA), an accounts representative at Warren Lanier Public Relations and as an A & R representative at RCA Records, Los Angeles, California.

Rose returned to Boston and along with record producer Maurice Starr became the primary architect of that, which in the late 70's and 80's would be called "The Boston Black Music Scene" a movement that ultimately led to the discovery of the international blockbusters Prince Charles and the City Beat Band, The Jonzun Crew, New Edition and New Kids on the Block. In 1979, he formed Solid Platinum Records and Productions. In the 80's, Rose held recording / production deals with Virgin Records, Atlantic Records and Pavilion / CBS/Sony Records

Tony Rose was a successful Executive Producer, Record Producer, Record Company Owner, Personal Manager, Music Publisher, Recording Studio Owner, Recording Engineer, Song Writer and Composer for more than fifteen years. His Solid Platinum Records and Productions was the first African American production company to have a production deal with Virgin Records. In 1983, albums produced by Rose "Gang War" and "Stone Killers" by *Prince Charles and the City Beat Band* reached Gold Album status and shared the charts with Michael Jackson's Thriller for six consecutive months in the number one, two and three positions throughout the world and his legendary "Prince Charles and the City Beat Band" albums "Gang War", "Stone Killers", "Combat Zone" and singles, have accounted for more than Four Million sold worldwide. Rose's many music awards include "Gold" and "Platinum" Albums and "Ampex Golden Reel" Awards for recording and engineering New Kids on the Block. Rose, has also penned Before the Legend – The Rise of New Kids on the Block and…A Guy Named Maurice Starr – The Early Years, published August 2008. WWW.TONYROSEENTERPRISES.COM

1
Funky Beginnings

What can I say about George Clinton? He is the most innovative rock and soul funkster on the planet, he has influenced a few generations of musicians in several music genres and he is *STILL* creating fresh grooves 60 years into his music career. His music interest started with his being a student of gospel, acapella singers and groups, street corner harmonies that moved the soul and lyrics that were spiritual and from the heart. George started his musical journey with his Doo Wop group, The Parliaments in the mid-1950's. The vocal harmonies and romantic ballads are what inspired him to form his own group.

Oh Yeah...........another motivator for George is that he learned that girls screamed and swooned over the guys in singing groups, so it paired his two loves: *music and the ladies*. As he grew to be a young man he studied and sat at the feet of young fledgling music artists, groups, writers, producers and moguls.

He would later learn the inner workings of the music industry as a songwriter and producer in the 1960's. His journey would help him continue to evolve through being a vocalist, songwriter, marketer, creator and futuristic master in the music industry. His was not an overnight success, but a path that has kept his career moving forward. In adapting new knowledge, he has been able to expand his career as an innovator, and artistic showman. George is still creating new music, touring and learning, collaborating with present day music artists and he has more projects in the works in 2017, 18, 19 and well into the 2020's.

His story starts in Kannapolis, North Carolina, a rural country area where Mr. George Edward Clinton, Jr. was born July 22, 1941. Kannapolis was a rural country area that is known for its textile industry. One of its early businessmen was a guy by the name James W. Cannon, who owned the county's largest manufacturing plant that made sheets and towels. The suburb is northeast of Charlotte. He says that his mother did not know she was pregnant with him, until she went to the bathroom; his entrance into the world began in a rural country *out house*. What a funky beginning! He is one of ten siblings.

His early memories of growing up start in Washington, DC. During World War II, his father was a serviceman coming home from the War. Many people migrated to the Washington Metropolitan Area for jobs during the War, most of them women. Talk of the atomic bomb seemed to be the topic of conversation as the" Bomb" was used in midsummer of 1945, the final year of World War II. In the book "Extended Play: Sounding Off -From John Gage to Dr. Funkenstein" author John Corbert interviewed George about his early life…George described his memories: "First time I can remember I was about five years old, my father had just come back from the service. The war was over; everyone was talking about the atomic bomb. I can remember the blackout, and big searchlights all over the sky at night. And in the daytime, you couldn't see the sky for rows and rows and rows of planes. I mean it literally had a top on it, all day every day."

Both of his parents, George Clinton, Sr. and Julious Keaton worked for the United States government. His Dad worked for the U.S. Mint and his Mom worked as a custodian at the Pentagon in Arlington, Virginia. When the war ended, his family moved to Chase City, Virginia. He played in the farm fields and went fishing with friends. His early childhood world was integrated. As children, he and his friends had no real understanding of racism.

After World War II, millions of blacks from rural and southern states migrated north for better employment, education and standard of living. Change was in the air when his father gained new employment opportunities and took young George and his siblings north to Newark, New Jersey, the state's largest city. His laid-back world of Virginia country life moved into the East Coast vibe, an exciting new direction. While traveling on the highways, gas stations signs, billboards, hotels, city life captured his young eyes for the first time. This new culture helped him to imagine and be opened to new possibilities that life would bring him.

George Sr. worked at the docks unloading goods from the ships. This strong work ethic was instilled in young George and his siblings. They all started learning the importance of responsibility, house chores and working at an early age. While the early introduction to working was not always fun, it did instill discipline for him. He respected his father's rules and his example as a strong role model. George Sr. was a church-going man who sang with gospel groups in the church congregation, but that was it. His work always kept him away and too busy for any music goal to flourish.

His mother Julious moved to nearby East Orange, New Jersey. In fact, she lived next door to the Reverend Mancel Warwick's grocery store. She loved traditional blues music, as well as rhythm

& blues, she had a passion for it. She sang to records by Wynonie Harris, Muddy Waters, B.B. King, and many others. George, Jr. made friend with the Warwick children: Dionne, Cissy, Dee Dee and the family. He even tried his hand at playing baseball with the neighborhood kids for fun, but he was not much of an athlete.

George grew up in an area named Clinton Hills in the South Ward. It was named after politician George Clinton, a former Governor of New York and Vice President of the United States under Presidents Thomas Jefferson and James Madison. He loved strutting along Clinton Avenue, the center of the area. He even graduated from a middle school called Clinton Place. He felt like as he puts it "royalty" growing up in that neighborhood. It greatly influenced his formal education and future musical aspirations.

George Jr. worked various jobs as a kid. He was a milk delivery boy; he even delivered milk to legendary jazz entertainer Sarah Vaughn. Later, he would find work on Clinton Avenue at a place called Essex Records. He would sweep up the store. Back then, if records did not sell well, they were not returned to the record company, they were trashed. As luck would find him, George created a new income for himself selling records from Essex that did not sell. He would micro-business selling the records from white music artists to white kids for fifteen cents each. Some records he kept for himself.

Early on, his music taste varied from the smooth ballads of the *Flamingo's* to the raw raucous rock & roll funk *of Jerry Lee Lewis* or *the Isley Brothers*! Their music hits *A Whole Lot of Shakin* a #1 hit September 9th through 16th in 1957 and *Shout* initially #47 on Billboard Pop Charts in 1959 embodied the energetic soulful funk along with amazing showmanship. *The Isley Brothers'* version of *Shout* would achieve RIAA Gold status over time. In 1999, it was inducted into the Grammy Hall of Fame and both of these songs are included in Rolling Stones 500 Greatest Songs of All Time.

It was in his early teens that George was hit by the music bug. His aunt Ruth lived in Passaic, New Jersey, next door to a member of a girl group called the *Shirelles*. She took him to see the young teen group led by Shirley Owens. The girls were working on a new song called *Mama Said*, it would become a top #5 hit for the group. In addition, he got to see the group's debut in 1953 when his aunt introduced him to the World-Famous Apollo Theatre in New York. Top R&B groups of the day like *The Drifters* and the *Chantels* were headlining with other music groups. The famous theatre was a major gig for any black artist wanting to make it big in the entertainment industry. Their audiences were very discriminating and quick to let an artist know if they got an ovation or yanked off stage! As George says: "I listened to them obsessively and loved them unconditionally." He would make many trips to this theatre to just enjoy and study popular artists of the day.

With the emergence of TV shows aimed at the teenage audience like **Bandstand** which was broadcast from Philadelphia Pennsylvania, and local amateur hour singing shows and feature films by popular disc jockey Alan Freed and other music personalities of the 1950's, kids got to see their favorite music performed by the groups that recorded the hits, both black and white. According to George, "You moved to what moved you." Race did not matter as a teen-age fan and consumer of fashion and music styles at that time. In fact, white culture got to hear rhythm & blues and George got familiar with some of the white music artists he loved that were influenced by black artists. It was the beginning of marketing rock and roll to teenagers and bringing kids from all walks of life together with a common goal, *enjoying the music.*

One thing that cannot be ignored is the racial and ethnic division of the times, the 1950's were still segregated. Black teenagers could not appear on Bandstand in the 1950's as part of the audience or dance on the show until the show left Philadelphia and went to California in the 1960's. There were other local teenage dance shows in the New York, New Jersey, Philadelphia and Delaware region that catered to a black audience. One successful example was *The Mitch Thomas Show, it* was a forerunner of the nationally syndicated

1970's show *Soul Train*. *The Mitch Thomas Show which* made its debut on August 13, 1955. It was broadcast out of Wilmington, Delaware on an unaffiliated station, WPFH, on Saturdays. His show influenced popular styles and dances that white kids would bring to *Bandstand*. The show also attracted the top black music talents of the day like *The Teenagers, Ray Charles, The Moonglows, Little Richard* and others.

Mitch had been a popular disc jockey on Philadelphia's WDAS; he worked with black radio legends *Jocko Henderson* and *George Woods*, who were popular disc jockeys in the Philadelphia/NJ area. But, it was Mitch who was given the TV show spot. Mitch, Jocko and George would hold regional amateur talent shows as well as live shows at local and popular venues like the *Uptown Theatre* in Philadelphia that featured national charting music stars. All the events would be integrated, and although there were more than a few local on-air talents, these three DJs were the most popular in the tri-region area; and black teens would have been introduced to and influenced by the music artists and their fashion and hair styles from the radio and live talent shows.

The Mitch Thomas Show had a successful three-year run. When the station was sold several years into his successful TV run, he had a tough time getting the national sponsors needed to remain on the air anywhere! WPFH was unaffiliated with a national TV network, and affiliated stations in 1958 were not easy to attract sponsors for a black teen dance show, even with national recording artists. Famous black music vocalists like: Lorenzo Fuller, who was the first to have a music variety show called "Man About Music" for NBC in 1947 and Billy Daniels who had his show on ABC-TV in 1952. Nate King Cole who had a show on NBC in the Fall of 1956 had that same issue in the 1950's, even when they had popular music stars, both black and white, on their shows and some product brand sponsorship. Because of Mitch's popularity, he did return to radio and local amateur talent shows after his TV show was canceled and remained a popular voice in the Philadelphia, Delaware and New Jersey radio market until the late 1960's.

Music on the radio in New Jersey included hits from many local artists from New York, as well as groups from the Mid-West. Some of George's early music influences and songs outside of gospel included: a group from Chicago, Illinois called The *Flamingos*, who sang: *"I Only have Eyes for You"* in 1959; *The Bobbettes*, a girl group from Spanish Harlem whose song *Mr. Lee* was a top #10 hit in 1957 and *The Spaniels*, led by singer Thornton James "Pookie" Hudson. They were from Gary, Indiana. The group recorded on the *Vee-Jay* label, one of the first and largest Black-American Record labels at the time. George was greatly influenced by Hudson's vocal style and stage presence. *The Spaniels'* famous signature song was *Good Night Sweetheart,* a hit for them in 1954. The group was also first to have its lead singer have his own microphone while the rest of the vocal group shared their own mic. The handsome group also impressed the ladies at live shows, the girls would scream in delight at these young men singing love songs to them. And George loved that singing meant getting the girls!

Groups like the *Spaniels* were inspired by the groups like the *Inkspots* from Indianapolis. The group with popular lead singer *Bill Kenny,* was a crossover group with R&B international hits in the 1930's and 40's. Another group to achieving mainstream popularity was the *Mills Brothers* from Piqua, Ohio. They were a jazz and pop quartet who sang in lush four-part harmony. The *Ravens* and the *Orioles* also expanded this genre with a more R&B style of singing with several tenors, a bass and a baritone singer in the late 40's and early fifties. The Doo Wop sound was made more distinct when the *Ravens* used their bass singer Jimmy "Ricky" Ricks as a trademark feature in their hits. This allowed the group to incorporate a variety of music genres that included Jazz, Pop, R&B and Gospel. Their style influenced many black groups that were popular in the fifties, as the bass singer was a must for many charting groups. In the book, *George Clinton & The Cosmic Odyssey of The P-Funk Empire* by author *Kris Leeds,* George says: "The fifties in New York was an incredibly romantic time to be brought up hearing that stuff. That was the music of your day. It was the music you fell in love to. I imagine it's like that for every generation, but here you had a soundtrack to your incredibly in-depth emotions of love. You combine that with being a teenager."

George would return to the Apollo often to enjoy the music of his favorite groups and discover new local talent such as Newark/Philadelphia group *The Blue Belles* led by powerful vocalist Patsy Holt. Others in the group were: *Sara Dash, Cindy Birdsong and Nona Hendrix.* George was Patsy and Nona's hairdresser. *The Bluebells* had a great success regionally in the 1960's. Patsy would later transform the group into a Funk Disco trio that would propel them into stardom. The group renamed themselves *Labelle.* The trio had a monster hit in 1974 called *Lady Marmalade.* Still later as *Patti Labelle,* she would have major solo artist's success on both the Billboard Soul and Pop Charts with hits like: *New Attitude, If You Asked Me To,* and *On My Own* with former *Doobie Brothers* turned solo vocalist *Michael MacDonald* in the 1980's.

The Newark area was ripe with young music talent to not only listen but to learn from and later to compete with. One group that George was especially taken with was *Frankie Lymon and the Teenagers.* In fact, because of his admiration of Pookie Hudson and *The Teenagers'* lead singer's harmonies, energy and popularity, at age 14 he was inspired to form his own group.

Frankie Lymon and the Teenagers had a major influence on teens across America. Frankie's voice, stage presence and *the Teenager* harmonies were magic. That influence was magnified on the East Coast as they inspired multiple teenage doo wop groups. Most wanted to be *The Teenagers,* some even adopting their monogrammed sweater, hairdo's and stage routines. *The Teenagers* were a group from Harlem. In the beginning, *Frankie* was not the lead singer. In fact, he was not even in the group. He became friend with the lead singer Herman Santiago of the Premiers in 1955. The members of the group were; *Herman Santiago, Jimmy Merchant, Joe Negroni and Sherman Gaines.* It was after the *Premiers* had a practice session with Frankie that he was invited to become a group member. Santiago was the lead singer and Frankie sang second tenor behind *Herman Santiago* and *Merchant* who were the writers of a love poem they renamed *Why Do Fools Fall in Love*. With a new hit in tow, the group attracted the attention of lead singer of the *Valentines, Richard Barett*. Barett was also a talent scout and producer of Rama Records. Richard introduced them to George Goldner, the label's owner. Goldner changed the group's name to *The Teenagers*; the song was released in January 1956. And it hit the top of the R & B music charts from March 17- April 7, 1956 and #6 on the Pop Singles Chart in America and #1 in Britain the summer of 1956. In fact, *The Teenagers* were the first American group with the honor of hitting #1 on the British charts.

Although *The Teenagers* had other hits like *Goody Goody* and *I Want You to Be My Girl*, label owner George Goldner started pushing Frankie to go solo. Neither the Teenagers nor Frankie had any further successful record releases apart that had the magic of the original group line-up. That spark, spontaneity of youth and fun that they had on television and in Alan Freed films like *Rock, Rock, Rock and Mr. Rock and Roll* was gone. But for that brief few years *Frankie Lymon and The Teenagers* had the ear and pulse of teenagers internationally. Frankie at 15 years old became hooked on heroin; his drug addiction destroyed his career, young adult life and ultimately ended his life February 27, 1968. He was only 25 years old.

The focus on Rock & Roll in the fifties was vocal harmonies, not bands. Occasionally music acts with flamboyant stage shows also played the Apollo. Jalacy Hawkins, famously known as *Scream n' Jay Hawkins,* was an American rhythm and blues musician, singer, songwriter and actor. His strong vocals, sung on his signature hit in 1956 called *"I Put a Spell on You",* his costumes of leopard skins and red leather and ghoulish stage props complete with a coffin and smoking skull is considered a pioneer in *"Shock Rock"*. This genre is something that George would help evolve and define in the 1970's. Although Hawkins did not hit the charts, his version of the song, is considered "one of the 500 Songs that shaped Rock and Roll" by *Rolling Stone Magazine.*

The focus for most Rock and Roll groups in the fifties was on vocal harmonies, not bands, but, *Singing!* It was a way for George and his new group to get attention from the girls, have importance in the community, etc. He and the boys now had to come up with a name. Culture and the media, like movies and TV shaped most teens' choices. The guys were influenced by the commercials, brands of liquor, cars, grooming products & cigarettes. The names of popular smokes stood out. The group settled on the name *The Parliaments.* The first group members were Charles Davis, Herbie Jenkins, Robert Lambert, Gene Boykins, and Gene Carlos. Within the first couple of years the group's personnel would change.

The early group line-up were members: *Grady Simon* and second lead singer *Fuzzy Haskins.* Before their first venture into the recording booth, another personnel change happened. Grady Thomas was fired to make room for *Calvin Simon.* He joined *Charles Davis, George Clinton, Robert Lambert and Herbie Jenkins.* One of the neighboring groups that the *Parliaments* were on a show bill with was *The Del Larks,* led by *Sammy Campbell.* His brother David formed the group in the 1950's while they were in high school. The group also included member *Berkeley Othello Noel,* a person who would serve as an inspiration for George and *Parliament* for a couple of decades. They too hung out with George and the *Parliaments* at the Silk Palace. Their first records were doo-wop songs released on George Blackwell's *Eastman Ea-Jay label.* They then put out a record on Atlantic. The singles included *"Bubblegum Doll"* and *"Lady Love"* in 1958-59, both regional hits. In the early 60's, Sammy wrote songs for George Blackwell's Smoke Records in Newark; but none were released and he was not paid. Even when Sammy left to start his music career at another label, Blackwell would block his record releases. Sammy also was a concert promoter in the region, he booked *The Parliaments* and the *Del Larks* as headliners for shows with other acts, such as *The Wonders*, a group that featured a young *Eddie Hazel*. Bass vocalist *Raymond Davis* was a member of the *Del Larks*, but left to join George's group in the early 60's.

Although no one in the group was a classical trained vocalist or musician, after much practice, the group became a popular act in the Newark area. What they lacked in understanding four or five part harmonies, they made up in showmanship. They even got invited to record with a local recording studio. They recorded songs *Poor Willie* backed with *Party Boys* in 1958. The single was released in 1959 on Hull Records and distributed on the *ABC-Paramount* label *APT*. But that single did not get much regional or national airplay. The Parliaments' next recordings were

Lonely Island b/w "You Make Me Wanna Cry on the Patterson, New Jersey Flipp label. Again, no real label promotion. They also recorded music made famous by Detroit doo-wop group *Nolan Strong & the Diablos*. Their best-known hits were *The Wind* in 1954 and *Mind Over Matter*. They were popular a decade before *Motown*, and had hits in the mid-fifties and early 1960's. The group's line-up included: *Nolan Strong, Juan Gutierrez, Willie Hunter, Quentin Eubanks*, and *Bob Edwards*, the lead singer who would influence a young Smokey Robinson. In addition, the *Diablos* made an impact on musicians in the genre of punk rock, and rock. The group recorded for Detroit-based Fortune Records.

Even with this slow dance from regional to national success, George knew that traditional school education could never replace his love for music. It just made him more determined to learn all that he could to make it. Other group studio time was done locally with independent labels and black labels Some of these record labels included popular *Chess* and *Vee-Jay Records* out of *Chicago*, and *King Records,* a *Syd Nathan's* company out of Cincinnati, Ohio. Some owners made a profit by selling their recordings to major distributors; this included the Parliament's first singles. Unfortunately for the group, this meant that they were cheated out of music royalties as artists and in George's case, royalties as songwriter and performer.

A plus side to the local record and recording companies is that they, along with independent record store owners could gauge the audience interest at the street level of a hit's potential. One of the first black-owned stores was in Harlem, called *Bobby's Record* store on 125th Street. The owner *Bobby Robinson* was an independent record producer and songwriter who produced hits like *Kansas City* for vocalist *Wilber Harrison* and the hit *Every Beat of My Heart* for *Gladys Knight and the Pips.* He also worked for a time with *Ahmet Ertegen,* founder and President of Atlantic Records. Having people like Bobby in the neighborhood let them be face to face to gauge what the consumers were buying. This gave local groups a chance to be heard and if they had successful airplay and sales, a more likely chance of getting to appear on amateur shows and tour regionally.

The Parliaments' first shows were at school dances, the YMCA, local talent shows and "Battle of the Groups" a regional singing battle of local talent that would include the *Four Seasons, The Monotones* and others. "You had two hours after the show to get your ass out of there," Clinton says. *The Four Seasons* came from the other side of Broad Street, where the Italians ran with a gang called the Barbarians and wore sagging trousers, like hip-hop kids would decades later. The teachers yelled at the white boys to pull their pants up. "We didn't know how they stayed up," Clinton says. "They had big belts, with the silver studs on them, which they'd take off and knock the shit out of you with." The black kids wore their own pants belted high, to look buff."

The World-famous Apollo could be intimidating for many artists because there were famous greats that played the place, as well as national budding artists that were super-talented. With much practice, The *Parliaments* were confident enough to appear. George said, "We won 'Amateur Night' at the Apollo so many times that we had to go on under different names."

In their neighborhood school, *The Parliaments* sang over the schools PA system as part of the high school announcements. George was a good student, but just did not feel that formal education was for him. He also was distracted by a familiar teenager's evolution: *love* and a cute teen named Carol Hall. She was a Parliament fan and thought he was hot! The love bug struck George away from the music scene for a bit, as he and Carol became an item. By his senior year, George was a father to a baby girl named Donna. Later that year, he had a son named George III. His life path changed so fast that he also needed to adapt to growing up faster than many of his peers, now that he had a family to support. His high school education stopped at the eleventh grade. At that time, his music career was not paying the bills 100%, so he turned his attention to becoming a successful songwriter and set out for New York City.

Multifarious Funk

2
Bootcamp and Entertainment Realities

In New York, his next journey in the music business gave him an opportunity to continue to learn from great songwriters and the music publishing companies. There were over 160 companies housed in the famous *Brill Building* located on Broadway and Fifty-Ninth Street in Manhattan. Yet along Broadway, there were other companies with budding songwriters like: *Jerry Leiber and Mike Stoller, Gerry Goffin, Carole King, Shaddow Morton, Barry Mann, Cynthia Weil, Phil Spector…* and the list goes on. Most of these songwriters began with *Aldon Music,* a company started by owner Don Kirshner and Al Nevins, located at 1650 Broadway and 51st Street. Most of the R&B and Rock music was recorded in the basement at Allegro Studios.

In the late 50's, George went to work for the Columbia Pictures-Screen Gems recording label Colpix. This label was founded in 1958 by Jonie Taps and Harry Cohn. Some of the popular label artists included: *Lou Christie, The Marcels, and Freddie Scott.* The labels' million selling hits were *The Marcels' Blue Moon* in 1961, and actress *Shelley Fabares'* hit with *Johnny Angel* in the summer of 1962. He learned not only how to write songs, but also how music moved people to love, cry, dance, and how a song was marketed. Songwriters fashioned songs for each group or solo act. Presentation, sound and marketing was an ensemble. That *"It Factor"* was what the songwriters were going for to help make their artists exciting to not only listen to but watch. George considered his time in Manhattan a *university education* in progress.

Promotion was also something that he learned. It was the element keeping the audience interested in the song. He was fascinated by how legendary producer *Phil Spector* would take out trade music paper ads in Billboard and *Cashbox* Magazine that advertised his next big music hits. These ads would go on for weeks. Phil kept his audience in anticipation because he would only reveal a mostly blank white page with a small portion of the artist's picture or album with a tease like: *Coming Soon and his music logo Spector Music.* The ad grew bigger week by week keeping his audience in suspense till the music singles debut. Only then could you see the full advertisement. These ads cost around $2,000 or more at that time.

George was attracted to the confidence of those music moguls that used innovative ways to advertise and use artists and music releases in a way that most were not. Another influence was singer *Richard Barnett* who was also a talent scout. He discovered artists like *Frankie Lymon and the Teenagers*, and *Little Anthony and the Imperials*. In addition, he worked with one of the first popular black girl groups the *Chantels*. They had a magical five-part harmony you hear in their classic hits: *He's Gone, Look in My Eyes* and the soulful ballad *Maybe*. Lead singer *Arlene Smith* was a classical trained vocalist who performed at Carnegie Hall at age 12. Arlene was the writer of *He's Gone* and thought to be an uncredited writer of the group's hit *Maybe*.

One of the first groups George worked with was a girl group from Northwest Washington D.C. called *The Jewels*. The group first recorded in legendary blues and R&B artist *Bo Diddley's b*asement recording studio. In the late 50's and early 60's Bo's career had taken him to international music stardom. He also had major media exposure in *Alan Freed's* popular Rock and Roll movies and European tour dates. He also was the music producer who recorded their debut album. The group's most well-known song was *Opportunity*, a moderate hit in 1964. Bo also recorded a young *Marvin Gaye* and *Moonglows* member *Harvey Fuqua*. After the

Jewels' lack of commercial success, they eventually became *James Brown's* backing vocalist in the mid 60's.

Studying the music charts was another thing George did. He would look at labels and see who was the producer or writer. Sometimes it was the same person. In the late 50's a songwriter named *Berry Gordy* was just starting to get some national exposure with his song *Lonely Teardrops* written for *Jackie Wilson*. *Curtis Mayfield* was also another writer that was a double talent as writer and producer writing *For Your Precious Love* for his group the Impressions. The lead on that song was *Jerry Butler,* but when Jerry left the group to go solo, Curtis took the lead on another hit song *Gypsy Woman* now a classic. George embraced both black and white writers and producers when studying their compositions and artist development. He followed his neighbor *Dionne Warwick* as composer Burt Bacharch helped shape hit songs for her distinctive vocal style.

The late *Sam Cooke* was also an inspiration to George. He came to George for haircuts several times. Sam was a very handsome, smooth, sophisticated ladies' man. In the late 1950's he sang with the gospel group, the *Soul Stirrers.* A young Sam's floating emotive tenor was a show-stopper on records and in live shows. In late 1957, he went solo with *You Send Me,* a crossover hit for him. He was an amazing songwriter and businessman, who would later become a success with his own record label called *SAR*, distributed by RCA Records. Sam produced other music groups like the *Valentinos* and solo artists like *former Highway QC's* tenor *Johnnie Taylor* with success that reached audiences internationally. In fact, one hit Sam produced for the *Valentinos* was re-recorded and turned into an international hit by British rockers the *Rolling Stones.* That song is *It's All Over Now,* was written by group member *Bobby Womack.*

Sam's crossover and multi-talented success in many areas made him a pioneer in the music industry. He inspired not only George, but *Smokey Robinson, Solomon Burke* and others. In about eight years in the music industry, Sam wrote and sang hits that made the ladies, both black and white, swoon and scream. He played the famous night club *Copacabana,* and was the first black artist to do so. He sang with singer Jackie Wilson and even recorded with heavyweight fighter *Cassius Clay*, later named *Muhammad Ali*. His career future looked great, and then in the month of December 1964, Sam was killed in a California motel by the manager who said it was in self-defense. George in hearing about the incident says, "It didn't add up to me then, and it still doesn't." He goes on to say:

"All I know for sure is how it affected us at the barbershop, and for that matter music fans everywhere. We were just numb all day long. It was like the Kennedy assassination a year earlier. In both cases, I was on the bus when I heard the news. I just kind of dropped down beneath it. I just blanked out. You can spend your time obsessing about the particulars of a situation, inventing conspiracies, questioning the official version- I've done plenty of that- but in the end, you come back to something more fundamental, which is that kind of sadness; that kind of subtraction, doesn't really belong in the world."

3
Fatherhood & Work Gigs

By 1960, George was now a father of three children. His education and working experience in New York was still not paying so George looked for more work in Newark. As luck would have it, a Wham O Toy plant was coming to town. So he and his neighborhood running buddies got jobs assembling the latest teenage craze: *Hula Hoops*! They were a popular craze nationally. In fact, so popular, the plant had a hard time keeping up with the demand. Ignoring child labor laws, George and his buddies would recruit local elementary school kids to help assemble the hoops. And their operations churned out so many hoops that they had to store a surplus in warehouses. He also had a side income from this. But as with any fad, that make-shift enterprise lasted only a short time. Wham-O moved their factories operation overseas.

His other vocational skill, to pay the bills, was as a hairdresser. He excelled enough to have quite a clientele in New Jersey alone to make good money. Straightening hair was the style in the late fifties and early sixties, for as George says: "Singers, Pimps and Preachers". Some of his famous clientele included *Jackie Wilson, Sam Cooke* and members of *The Temptations*. He made a few hundred dollars a week which was excellent income in those days. In Newark, he had steady employment, yet the city was becoming very poverty stricken. By the late 50's the city lost manufacturing job opportunities as factories moved out of the city. In the ten years that he had lived there in Newark, population had dropped by almost half a million. He tired of that area and sought work in Plainfield, New Jersey. George felt it would be better for his career. Plainfield in the early 1960's had a bit more middle class clientele, better education and more employment opportunities. In certain parts of the city, some working class over lapped with the wealthy, country transplants, and poor. There was still crime in the city, but it was a step up from Newark.

In its heyday, Plainfield was a regional shopping and entertainment center. Residents of nearby Union, Middlesex and Somerset counties would drive in to shop and explore the business districts of Plainfield. Other than during the holidays, peak shopping times in Plainfield were Thursday nights and Saturday, when Front Street and the areas around it bustled. Parking spots were at a premium downtown during the fifties and early sixties, including at major department store and upscale boutiques. Plainfield had plenty of entertainment venues. At the peak, there were four operating movie theaters: *the Strand, the Liberty, the Paramount and the Oxford theaters*. Prior to 1960, Cedarbrook Park, at the south end of town, and *Greenbrook Park,* at the north end of town, provided every opportunity for recreation, including ice skating in the winter, fishing, hiking, visits to the ice cream vendor, playgrounds and quiet walks.

In his new barbershop, George soon had the most customers in a shop of both young and old patrons. With this show in leadership, he was soon the manager of the shop, taking 25 cents from each barber in the shop and he made five dollars a customer by doing "Do's". He changed the shop's decor and attracted more young clients. Most mature clients wanted to stay with conservative haircuts and "Do's"; but George's specialty hair-do was the Quo Vadis, a close high and tight style most of the young hip guys wore. That style required hair grease! In Spanish, the term meant "Where are you going?" Another style was finger waves and the conk style that used heavy chemicals. His advertising included a picture of him. As he stayed so busy, George rarely had time to do his own hair. One of his ads read, 'Come get your hair done or you could end up looking like me'.

The love of music never left George though. His new gig as manager of a place he renamed T*he Silk Palace* made him financially stable enough so he could invest some money into his music career. The *Parliaments* were checking out other groups in the neighborhood as well as the surrounding cities in New Jersey. There was always something new to learn to remain relevant in the music scene, and become one of the top contenders for regional gigs with more opportunities to record their own music. In the late 50's his music goals were also changing from a local influence to a more national one.

In Plainfield, he not only looked at vocal groups, but a new group of musicians that were making a splash in the New Jersey region. Some of these guys would be patrons of George's barbershop. It had become a neighborhood hangout for young ideas and a safe social hub away from rough street life for young kids and teens. He made many life-long friends there. The nucleus of new group members also evolved at the shop. Members of the future P-Funk like *Cordell "Boogie Mosson, Garry Shider, Eddie Hazel, Bernie Worrell and Eddie "Bass" Nelson* all came by and hung out at the Silk Palace.

Multifarious Funk

4
Labels and Liaisons

By the early 1960's, George was paying attention more to a music label owner, songwriter, and producer named B*erry Gordy*. He read music labels to see who was who in the music scene and who was producing the records. Berry, originally a record shop owner who sold jazz music, also worked at the Lincoln-Mercury car plant in Detroit. He was also a songwriter that had recent success writing songs for singer *Jackie Wilson*. Some songs that became national hits included: *"Reet Petit"* and a major chart hit *"Lonely Teardrops"*.

With profits from songs recorded by Wilson, Gordy was able to start Tamla Records and started to build a roster of recording artists. In the beginning, Mr. Gordy distributed his music with other established labels like U*nited Artist Records* and *Chess,* but within a couple years and asking his family for money to start his own business, he formed *Motown Records Corporation,* located on 2648 West Grand Boulevard. *Motown* had its own music artists, musicians, housed its own music labels and a publishing company called *Jobette*. In fact, if a song became a hit, crossover artists like *Frank Sinatra, Tony Bennett or Mitch Ryder* would also cover some of the hits that came from the label's songwriters. This made more cash flow for the label. Motown was also more than a music label; it began to shape pop culture early on. It tapped into young America across racial lines and helped bring people together.

George was very impressed with Berry and a young songwriter at the label named *Bill "Smokey" Robinson*. He was lead singer of a group called the *Miracles*. He called Smokey a triple threat: a songwriter, singer and producer who could mold music hits to whatever vocal artist or group he was working with. He was so taken with what Motown was doing that he and the *Parliaments* decided to go to Detroit to not only see their favorite artists but to audition for the label. They had consistently won amateur nights at the *Apollo* and around their region. The group drove to Detroit and arrived early in front of Motown headquarters; they were amazed by the arrival of the label's artists that walked across the front lawn. After George and his crew took a look at themselves, a wake-up call back to reality settled in. They were not dealing with a local, regional mix of musicians; they now were faced to face with chart-hitting acts that had been polished to compete internationally. Although they were intimidated, they pressed on to tour the place and meet artists, producers, band members and others in the company.

The person to lead them around was *Martha Reeves,* who started out as a secretary, then a back-up singer for *Marvin Gaye.* She would go on to have popular success with her own group *The Vandellas. The Parliaments* got an audition, but were turned down. In George's quest for stardom, his group sounded too much like others in the Motown stable. Another factor was presentation; the group did not have a distinct look the label was going for. So George briefly became a songwriter for the label. He would commute between Plainfield to Detroit on weekends. One songwriter he met there was *Sidney Barnes* who had briefly been a vocalist for Motown. He was a handsome man who was business partners with *Berry Gordy's* first wife *Raynoma. Raynoma* was a great businesswoman who worked to make *Jobette Music, Motown's* publishing branch, a success. George worked with her for a brief time until Berry merged *Jobette Music* into *Motown. Raynoma's* impression of a young George Clinton in 1963 when he came to work from the label: "This guy had great potential; He's also clean cut, soft spoken with a beautiful smile. Tailored pin-striped suits and a briefcase."

The world was in a state of change and the music industry followed. The vocalist and vocal groups of the day like *the Ronettes, Gary U.S. Bonds, Shangri-Las, The Angels, Shirelles, Bobby Darin,* the

Drifters and others were being challenged on their home turf by changing times. The theme of love, romance and innocence, and fun songs shifted as the Vietnam War, Kennedy Assassination and Civil Rights confrontations and killings filled the newspapers and evening news. About the same time, the British invasion happened. George listened and just observed what they were doing musically as writers and composers. He could see the groups had a sincere love of American Rhythm and Blues. The *Beatles* and *the Rolling Stones* had even recorded some songs originally made famous by the *Isley Brothers and Bobby Womack*. Their versions of these cover hits sold into the millions and exposed white American kids to the rhythm and blues music that their parents would not have accepted by black artists.

The British groups, however, also wrote their own hits, and created a fashion and culture craze that greatly impacted the music industry. For every American group that was famous in the mid- sixties there were as many groups from the U.K that dominated the charts. You also had folk artists like *Bob Dylan* and trios like *Peter, Paul and Mary* whose lyrics inspired many to think and make a move to change cultural and government barriers blocking equal rights for blacks and women; politically, economically and socially. The music scene changed almost overnight from the Doo Wop groups that only harmonized and sang love songs, to message music that reflected the changing times.

Most vocal groups were being replaced by music groups with triple skills as writers, musicians and sometimes producers. Hits from R&B artists like *Curtis Mayfield and Sam Cooke* had their social message hits *People Get Ready* and *A Change is Gonna Come* in 1964-65 impacting the music landscape. Some black artists like *James Brown, Wilson Picket, Dionne Warwick, Jerry Butler, Curtis Mayfield and Aretha Franklin* inspired the Brits and remained on the American, U.K. and international charts. Doo Wop favorites - *The Dells and The Platters, Little Anthony and the Imperials* - were also able to break through with updated styles and hits in the mid-sixties. But the music company with a roster of artists that was able to survive this British Invasion was *Motown Records*.

In Detroit, George was learning from the industry giants, but it did not allow him creative development. To remain current, companies always looked for the newest groups, musicians and trends. For George as an artist, he was looking to grow his industry knowledge and use his skills; so he kept himself opened to new opportunities outside Motown. The city also became a new home to new independent record labels and young artists looking to make their break into the already competitive field. It also attracted seasoned artists wanting to revive and update their music brand. *Motown* attracted young teenage songwriters and a future funkster to record their first recordings. *Neil Young and Ricky Johnson* aka *Rick James with The Mynah Birds* recorded for Motown in the mid-sixties and a couple of members would go on to other groups like *Crosby, Stills, Nash and Young* and the keyboard player joined up with *Steppenwolf* and British singer *Kiki Dee*. TV star *Paul Peterson* of the *Donna Reed* Show and vocalist *Meatloaf* recorded for Motown too. However, the label was not the place for these artists; because young artists, even though they knew what their generation was listening to, could not fully produce their own compositions. Most, except Ricky Johnson, would go on to greater music and career success in the late 60's and into the 70's with other labels. Ricky Johnson would stay off and on as a songwriter/musician with Motown, and finally in the late 70's would achieve legendary status as Rick James.

On one of his weekend trips, George met a business mogul named *Ed Wingate*. He was one of the richest and well-respected black businessmen in Detroit. He owned a lot of real estate, taxicab companies, hotels, supper clubs and record labels. Mr. Wingate was not a natural musician, but he was approached by *Berry Gordy* after The Miracles' song *Shop Around* became a major national multi- million selling hit for Motown. The company was having trouble keeping up with demand for the record, so Gordy invited

Wingate to the studio to tour and to become a partner in business. But Wingate decided after looking over Berry's label success to start his own music enterprise. Although not a natural musician, he had the charisma, connections, success sense in business to recruit the best, and the *cash flow* to pay for it.

A friendship grew between George and Wingate and soon a new career opportunity developed for him that would help utilize his early education in Manhattan's music district. He and *Sidney Barnes* would leave Motown to join Wingate and his business partner *Joanne Bratton*. Joanne, a beautiful cover girl model and former wife of welter weight boxer *Johnny Bratton* was a sharp business woman. She, Wingate, and Mr. Wilbur Golden founded *Golden World* in 1965. They helped shape several independent record labels: Ric-Tic, Wingate, and Revilot Records. She and Mr. Wingate had some success at their labels with groups like: *The Reflections*, who had a hit *Just Like Romeo and Juliette* in 1964. This was the company's national breakout top 10 hit.

Another of the groups was *The Shades of Blue,* who had the hit *Oh How Happy You Have Made Me* in 1965 and *Cool Jerk* by the *Capitols*. This hit was co-written by label song writer and singer *Edwin Starr*. One of his personal break-out hits in the mid-sixties was *Double-O Soul*. Edwin would go on to have a major success as a recording artist on Motown Records. Original offices for *Golden World* were located on 3246 West Davidson. The studio was state of the art, and soon attracted artists, top songwriters, producers, and even some of Motown's *Funk Brothers* who moonlighted there for additional income.

Early in their business collaboration, Mr. Wingate would fly George to Detroit. He became a songwriter for his record labels. This experience allowed George the room for creativity to not only write songs, but learn how to pull out all the previous experience he'd learned to use. It was *a boot camp* of sorts for him to learn, grow, fail, regroup and rework his skills as a writer, producer, promoter

Multifarious Funk

and company networker. This new role although exciting was hectic, but he loved working for Mr. Wingate.

In the beginnings of his work with Wingate, he would stay at his impressive home in the Edison District in Detroit. The District is known for having elegant homes and large mansions. It was and still is home to famous wealthy residents, like automobile creator *Henry Ford, William Metzger* of *Cadillac, William Kresge* founder of *S.S. Kresge*, later K-mart, and record company mogul *Berry Gordy*. Today the Edison District is one of the largest historical districts in the nation and is listed on the National Register of Historic Places.

Early music collaborations and recordings were done at Wingate's home before he built his Recording Studio on West Davidson in 1965. By early 1966 Golden World grew an impressive list of artists like the *Fantastic Four, J.J. Barnes, Flaming Embers, San Remo Strings* and a vocalist named *Theresa Lindsey*, from Romulus, Michigan. Wingate, always one to listen to what was going on in the city, had an idea of what he wanted George to do next. Upon hearing a local DJ *Martha Jean "The Queen" Steinberg*, program director of CKLW in Windsor, Ontario, who had catchphrases that became popular to Detroit radio listeners, he convinced George to write a song using one of these phrases in Theresa's new hit. George wrote it and *Theresa Lindsey* even contributed some lines to it. That song titled *I'll Bet You* was released in 1966. *Mike Terry* was the arranger and *Dennis Coffey* did his distinct guitar work on this single.

While working for Eddie Wingate, if George was not staying at Ed's home, he would stay at one of the popular hotels he owned with business partner Ernest Mackey, the *20 Grand Motel* which opened the summer of 1966. The Motel was the talk of the society pages, locally and nation. It was described as a half-a-million-dollar property with plush interior rooms and it even had a Penthouse on the top floor that had two three-bedroom suites. The gossip pages described "The big open house" that Detroit sportsman-businessman Ed Wingate and Ernest Mackey had at the opening of their big plush motel. But what visitors were awed at was Wingate's room which was done all up in the brightest red decor: red walls, red ceilings, red rugs, red drapes, red bedspread, etc."

Whoa!!

It was located adjacent to the popular *20 Grand Nightclub,* one of the most celebrated clubs in Detroit. It was where all the music acts, including Motown artists like: Little Stevie Wonder, The Contours, Chuck Jackson, Supremes, Temptations; Golden World artists' Edwin Starr, and George and the Parliaments would play many times. In an article in the Michigan Chronicle called *Remembering the 20 Grand, Detroit's Most Celebrated Nightclub,* it describes the place as: "Owned by Bill Kabbush and Marty Eisner, the 20 Grand opened its doors in 1953. For the rest of that decade and through most of the 1960s it was the place to go. But, of course, you had to "get sharp" first. It was a beautiful place. There was the Driftwood Lounge and the Fireside Lounge. Above the bowling alley was the Gold Room, a premier reception room that sat 1,200. Virtually all the top stars of the day performed at the 20 Grand, generally doing a week or two-week stint. Popular Detroit DJ the great *"Frantic Ernie Durham',* one of the kings of Detroit radio emceed. Earlier, many shows were emceed by Ziggy Johnson, a Detroit tap dancer who, like Durham, is a legend." *November 16, 2010.*

Golden World became a rival to *Motown* in terms of record airplay. Although the label existed for only six years, it made impact with many national hit records. This success alarmed Berry Gordy because many of his musicians would moonlight at Golden World for extra money, and their music sound trade marks were on the rival labels hits. Even though the musicians would get hit in the pocket financially with fines from Motown, Wingate would pay their penalties and keep them working. Finally, in late 1966, Berry offered Ed about a million dollars for the label, and he sold it to him in 1967. Wingate still held on to *Ric-Tic* records. With the sale to Golden World, Berry gained the artists' roster and the music publishing catalog. The artists' roster included: *Edwin Starr, The Fantastic Four, J.J. Barnes, The Dynamics later renamed the Dramatics*. The acquisition did not include the writing team *Geo-Si, Mik,* short for *George Clinton, Sidney Barnes* and *Mike Terry,* a saxophonist for Motown or vocalist Pat Lewis. Some artists refused contracts offered to them by Motown. With a solid roster of stars on the label already, some artists from Golden World felt they would not get their fair opportunity on the label.

5
Lasting Connections and Transforming Genres

Sidney Barnes and George remained friend and collaborators in the music business for decades. Sidney had credits on hit singles and albums by artists like: *B.B. King, Shangri-Las, The Jackson 5, The Supremes* and he would additionally collaborate with George on the *Parliament* mega-hit albums like *The Mothership Connection* and other platinum *P-Funk* albums.

In 1967, *Sidney* joined *Marshall Chess, Charles Stepney,* and *Minnie Riperton*, forming a Psychedelic/Soul band called *Rotary Connection*. Minnie Riperton and *Sidney Barnes* were the group's lead singers. The group recorded classic albums for *Chess Records* and toured the US, opening for top rock and blues act of the day like" *B.B. King, The Rolling Stones, Janis Joplin, The Doors, Led Zeppelin, Sly and The Family Stone, Moody Blues and Jefferson Airplane*. Although the group disbanded in 1970, their impact on future 1970's artists like *Elton John and Maurice White, Donny Hathaway and Chaka Khan* are a testament to the bands influence from their music productions, on the future artist superstars of the 1970's.

Sir Elton John said in a *Billboard Magazine* interview years ago that, "When he heard what *Charles Stepney* (Rotary's arranger and producer) had done musically with *Rotary Connection,* he knew that he could mix classical music with rock music and make it work". *Maurice White, a* drummer for the *Ramsey Lewis Jazz Trio,* was planning to form his own band and *Rotary Connection* influenced him "On that very day I realized what type of group I wanted to form, and what direction they would take." Rotary inspired *Earth Wind & Fire* and Maurice also took Charles Stepney, Rotary's arranger and producer, and then adopted Rotary's recording style and live visual stage concept to complete his vision.

Innovation, collaboration and ability, re-imagining a genre and an ensemble group, these are some music traits both Sidney and George shared in their business relationship. They would continue from time to time to collaborate on *Parliament's* platinum selling albums and Sidney would also join George and the P-Funk Bands on stage through the next few decades.

George also worked with vocalist *Pat Lewis*. She hailed from Johnstown, Pennsylvania but grew up in Detroit. She was in the group *The Adorables*, and also did back-up vocals for artists at Golden World. She also filled in for one of Motown's famous back-up group's *Andantes* on *Stevie Wonder's* 1966 hit *"Uptight"*. The song was #3 on the Billboard Charts. She also sang back up for *George and The Parliaments, Aretha Franklin and Isaac Hayes.*

As Motown's acquisition of Golden World was happening, George was gearing up to record the first single he wrote called *'I Wanna Testify"*. Wingate let George and *Pat Lewis* record this single on *Lebaron Toliver's* record label, *Revilot*. Lebron was also a radio DJ with connections in the music industry. The single also included a fifteen-year-old *Ron Banks* joining *Pat Lewis*. Banks was a member of the singing group *The Dramatics*. George was the only *Parliament* group member flown to Detroit to cover lead vocals. The song became a national top twenty hit in 1967.

Before national success, George and the band lived on the road. It put a strain on his marriage to high school sweetheart Carol and his family in Newark. When George worked for Mr. Wingate he was discouraged from having relationships with the ladies at *Golden World*. But that did not prevent him from having other love relationships outside his marriage with ladies on the road. He would have about fourteen children over the years. In addition, to his children with his first wife, he also had other kids with various partners.

After *I Wanna Testify* almost immediately hit the top 10 in Detroit, *The Parliaments* were on the road to promote their new hit. They played the regional and national teen scene. One of those gigs was at the *Apollo Theatre* where they headlined over the *O'Jays*. George would learn from this experience playing at various venues, using union musicians not skilled in R&B music that he needed to have a backing band to compliment his musical vision and the group's evolving style. In this growth, George felt that *Parliament* was out of touch with the times and the new music he was hearing. He was being guided by his audience of young teens and college aged fans.

6
Canceled By 2 Riots, Parliaments Undaunted

An article of the times read. "The Parliaments like that comedian, must be declaring, "If we didn't have bad luck, we wouldn't have any." After cutting *I Wanna Testify* for Detroit-based Hit Bound Records, and watching it slowly but steadily climb the charts, the Newark, N.J. natives were all set to do their stuff in their home town when two days before the scheduled performance, the riot broke out and the theatre in which they were to appear burned down. Their car was totally destroyed by the fire in front of the theatre, and their uniforms were consumed by flames in gutted cleaning establishment. Undaunted, The Parliaments caught a plane headed for Detroit and another theatre engagement. In the middle of that seven-day engagement, a riot broke out in Detroit and the show was canceled. The group picked up a new Cadillac El Dorado in the Motor City and headed back East, confident that bad luck was finally behind them. Then it happened. Their brand-new car hit a slick spot on a rain-swept highway and the vehicle was demolished. No one was injured. The Parliaments hopped a bus- and made their appearance on time. Said leader George Clinton: "You can't keep a good bunch down."

The first tour they did was with popular Philadelphia group *The Delfonics* who at the time were charting national hits. He says: "We did our first tour with them, when we were the *Parliaments*. We got along good. "It was also an education for The Parliaments to tour and learn from new music and culture that was changing in the late 1960's. Russ Terrana who had been with Golden World until it was bought by Motown in 1967, became chief studio engineer at Motown. In 1967, The Parliaments were evolving artistically, Russ recalls the new George: "The first few times I ran into George and the band in the studio, which was before I was working for Golden World, they looked like a group of insurance salesmen, dressed in those conservative coats and ties." But by the summer of 1966, the band decided to start altering their image. "They came in for a session, dressed very bizarre, like gypsies. George Clinton was wearing a Kotex around his neck like a scarf! It was totally off the wall. The tracks we recorded that day had a different feel than what I had heard from the group before."

In one of their first TV appearances, The Parliaments appeared in this segment in Hippie dress and sang a medley of songs *including I Wanna Testify, What is Soul?* The *Parliaments* harmonized, *George* withered on the floor and *Eddie w*ailed on guitar. In later appearances, their new stage look took on an individual look with each member of the band wearing a different costume such as hippie garb, bell bottoms, a suit, the American flag and George wearing a diaper, a sheet or nothing at all. Their stage shows became a new psychedelic experience.

The new Parliament music was not easily received by music critics though. *The Parliaments'* sound and look completely changed from its original niche' George says: "We were too white for black folks and too black for white folks." The fans at the college level could get where the band was going with their message and that was what the band wanted – to define a new music niche for themselves with no compromises to please the status-quo.

Multifarious Funk

7
Age of Hippie Change

In the mid-sixties, music started to take on a more political stand due to the continuing war, political, social and racial tensions. Most of these events were being played out on live TV, on college campuses and neighborhoods all over the country. American's and the world could see the political turmoil, the space discoveries and landings, riots with students and police, prominent leaders killed, Vietnam updates, civil rights marchers clashing with police. The counter culture movement was in full swing in the late 60's, as students - many from middle class backgrounds - began to question the social norms that they were taught by their parents, church and society. Freedom Riders, Civil Rights Supporters, Hippies, Environmentalism, Labor Movements, Peace Demonstrators, Anti War Demonstrators, Draft Dodgers, The Black Muslim Movement, and the Black Panthers Flower Power Movement all influenced social change.

In terms of the Traditional American morals of Christianity, and wholesome portrayal of family values, the Hippie Movement promoted the birth control pill, public nudity, expressions of alternate forms of sexuality, avant-garde art, revealing nude fashions, Psychedelic music and films all promoted this growing wave of lifestyle. It was a communal way of being. People shared love, drugs, food, and homes. Art was a spontaneous expression. Its creators were given time and freedom to create without constraint.

The drug culture became a way of life for much of young America. Marijuana, LSD and recreational drugs were promoted by Dr. Timothy Leary and psychedelic rock musicians as a way to raise consciousness. George and the band were users of coke and marijuana, but when they hit the Boston music scene, LSD was the groupie's drug of choice. Of course, George and the band experimented with it, but that high wore off after a few years. George admitted "It changed my mind about a lot of things to the positive, helped me get out of the mentality of clawing and scratching and fighting over everything, and being jealous of everything. It helped us try new things that we wouldn't have ever tried before. But that part of it was over in 1970. To me, Woodstock ended, and you had to start over again. By *Chocolate City*, and then *Mothership Connection*, we had a whole 'nother outlook. Now it's a spaceship with lots of expensive costumes as opposed to diapers and sheets."

The time considered the *"Summer of Love"* had a mix of non-traditional or straight soul, pop and rock music genre topping the Billboard charts internationally. Music in the late sixties pushed a hit single past the usual two and a half minutes. George was inspired by the *Beatles*. *"Yellow Submarine"* inspired him as well as *Sly Stone* and *Curtis Mayfield*. George said: But when I want to get inspired, I always listen to the *Beatles* shit" That'll always wake your ass up."

8
Loads of Musical Potpourri

Popular hit singles could also have incorporated elements of the classical composers, gospel and jazz experience of the late 40's and 50's. The compositions in the late sixties could include an interpretation of classical music like *Procol Harem's Whiter Shade of Pale*. The 1967 song starts with an amazing organ solo inspired by *Johann Sebastian, Bach's* composition *"Air on the G String*. Music also featured soloist in the music, *Jimi Hendrix*, an early 60's backup band musician for *James Brown and Little Richard*, he became a major star because of his guitar solos. Iron Butterfly's mega hit *In-A-Gadda-Da-Vida* rocked the airwaves at almost twenty minutes in 1968. *James Brown* called out his band soloist in hits like *Papa's got a Brand-New Bag i*n 1965. The *Rolling Stones* also experimented with baroque laced numbers like *She's Like a Rainbow* in 1967. *The Bee Gees* crossed classical and blues with their late sixties major hit *Got to Get a Message to You* in 1968. *Steppenwolf,* a Canadian-American group dropped a funky #3 Billboard hit with psychedelic sounds, rocking organ and soulful bass line on '*Magic Carpet Ride"* in 1968.

George's taste in music was quite broad: "Oh, my God, they (*Creedence Clearwater Revival)* was one of my favorites," he exclaims. "I always wondered where the fuck did they come from 'cause they were so funky and then I found out they were from California!"

An unlikely song with ambiguous lyrics partnered with an orchestrated composition sung by actor *Richard Harris* called *"MacArthur Park"* topped the charts in 1968; Detroit rocker *Bob Seger* also had a funky national hit called *Ramblin Gamblin Man* in

1968; the Memphis soul jazz influenced mixes with cheering chants on the hit *"Soul Finger"* by the teen group *The Bar-kays*. It cracked the top #20 in the summer of 1967, and *Sly Stone* dominated and influenced the music scene in the late 60's. Sly took his talent forward as the leader of his band *Family Stone*. The song *Dance to the Music* went up the Billboard R & B charts to #3 and #20 on the pop chart. All his band mates got vocal and instrumental solos on the pop and soul infuse hit in 1968. George had his first nationally charting hit during this time with *"I Wanna Testify* in 1967. And he did it with an independent black label owned in Detroit! George says, "White groups had done blues, and we wanted to head back in the other direction, to be a black rock group playing the loudest, funkiest combination of psychedelic rock and thunderous R & B."

Sly Stone was born Sylvester Stewart, he hailed from Denton. While growing up in a strict religious family, he and his siblings sang gospel music. A child prodigy, he was able to master several instruments by the age of twelve. His journey in the music business started in San Francisco as a disc jockey at KSOL. Sly would later start producing music artists on Autumn Records for area bands. His early success as a record producer was for the folk-rock group called *The Beau Brummels*. The groups debut single *"Laugh Laugh"* hit # 15 on the charts in February1964. In 1965, Sly produced the bands follow-up hit *"Just A Little"*. The bands song writer Ron Elliott credits Sly with "pulling a lot of loose ends of the band together."

Sly formed the interracial group The Family Stone in 1966. The group included: *Cynthia Robinson on Trumpet, Larry Graham on bass, Gregg Errico on drums, Jerry Martini on Saxophone, Freddie Stone on lead guitar, Rosie Stone on keyboards.*

They were signed to CBS's Epic Records in 1967. With the praise of rock critics and jazz great *Tony Bennett* they got the attention of *Clive Davis* who asked Sly to make his music more commercial. Chart success followed and *"Dance to the Music"* topped the pop charts and an album followed. The group had other top 10 hits like: *"Everyday People"* a #1 Billboard hit in 1968; the album *"Stand"* sold more than 3 million copies "a single *"Hot Fun in the Summertime"* peaked at #2 on the Billboard charts in 1969. With all of his success, Sly had spent a lot of his time getting too high to make his concert gigs.

George loved Sly as a peer and an innovator. They met in the late 60's when George and his band were signed to Sly's label *Stone Flower*. Nothing was ever produced on the label though. In the late seventies, the friends reconnected. Sly moved to Clinton's farm in Michigan for a year. They spent their days fishing, freebasing and recording music. Back in the Sixties, Clinton says, Sly was a prime influence, a person who showed him the myriad possibilities for R&B, that it could be slick and psychedelic all at once. "It could be anything you needed it to be," Clinton says. *"Hot Fun in the Summertime* was a knife." In the studio, Clinton watched Sly do everything backward, recording a high-hat cymbal part first, then a snare drum, then playing bass. "You don't know what the fuck he's hearing in his head," Clinton says. "But in his mind, he'd already wrote the arrangement, and he knows where everything is." - Rolling Stone

9
Detroit's Shock Rock

At his second home in Detroit in the late 1960's, the punk and soul music scene was growing in popularity, especially with the teen and college fans. George studied and toured with *Iggy Pop and the Stooges,* Iggy was born James Newell Ostenberg Jr. in Muskegon, Michigan. He started playing drums in local blues bands in Ann Arbor, his band was called the *Iguana's.* His stage name is said to come from this group. Iggy's on-stage persona was inspired by *James Brown, MC5 and the Doors* front man *Jim Morrison.*

Iggy's on stage antics included unpredictable behavior including stripping and diving into the audience, his music defines itself as a cross between rock, blues, and funk. It's a genre all its own…….. A punk niche. An "in your face" message set to hard rock". *Iggy Pop's* innovative influence would attract imitators and fans and new bands for decades into the millennium.

"We always [hung out with] the same "Bad Boys of Ann Arbor" crew. Amboy Dukes, Ted Nugent, Iggy and the MC5. And we'd just bullshit, we would try to come up with all kind of ways. So it was always about theatrics," Iggy said. "We ought to get married. That would make a nice crazy-ass story."

George was managed by the same Ann Arbor agency that handled *Mitch Rider and the Detroit Wheels* and *MC5*. He, the band and Iggy would hang out. George was influenced by him saying that his diaper wearing punk persona is "Just a funky notion". Back then it was, like, psychedelic into punk – Iggy Pop was running with us. It was about rudeness, at that point. So we did the same

Multifarious Funk

thing, but we did it with a joke. I knew it was outlandish. We just said, "Let's be stupid with it."

Another of George's influences around this time was *The Mothers of Invention* with lead singer *Frank Zappa*. The group had an amusing stage show, message and changing group line-up. This California group was a part of the underground scene in the late 1960's. Members included *Roy Collins, Roy Estrada, Zappa. Jimmy Carl Black, and Elliot Ingber.* In 1966, the band had their debut album called *"Freakout"* on the *Verve label*.

The group would undergo many lineup changes. Some other prominent members would include the *Turtles'* lead singer *Howard Kaylan and Mark Volkman, Turtles'* bassist Jim Pons, and on keyboards, George *Duke*. The group's sound could be a mix of orchestral and jazz, but could also move into other music styles. The lyrics mocked the norms of society and questioned pop culture and conformity. The group's shows were music theater and their album images satirized the hippie, flower power movement, even the *Beatles Sgt. Pepper's Lonely Hearts Club Band"* album cover.

That album *"We're Only in It for the Money"* released in 1968. The Mothers' original cover features a group collage that included *Jimi Hendrix*. Their record label was afraid of lawsuits so they included the cover artwork on the inside. Zappa was not happy but the album hit the Billboard top 30. In 2005, the album was included in the National Recording Registry.

George *was* impressed with *MC5*, they were considered the loudest, brashest, most progressive band. Their members included lead vocalist *Rob Tyner, Wayne Kramer and Fred "Sonic" Smith on guitars, Michael Davis on Bass, and Dennis Thompson* on drums. They were even featured in a cover story in January 1969 in *Rolling Stone Magazine*, this before their album debut. Their music style was a mix of blues, hard rock and psychedelic rock. They too, had an over the top stage show which could include rifles. The band used their guitars to imitate their favorite free-jazz artists like *Sun Ra,* an artist also known for his experimental music brand of "cosmic philosophy" and theatrical stage shows.

MC5 was also politically progressive, supporting far left protest social movements like the, Anti-War Movement. George and *Funkadelic* toured with them and it brought a clash of two cultures and treatment from law enforcement, one black and one white. George and the band were drug users, but *MC5* were a confrontational group of users. On one group tour their loud members attracted the police who searched *Funkadelic* first. Members of the group were searched and marijuana was found on both groups, but the *Parliaments* were busted. It was *MC5* who caused the major disruption on the plane from the beginning. "We were all trying to push music ahead, to break out of the three-minute pop-song idea and expand it," says *MC5* guitarist Wayne Kramer. "I remember thinking, 'Those guys are doing the same thing we're doing, except we're coming from a rock background and they're coming from funk.' I would put George right there with any of the great bandleaders, Miles or 'Trane. Songs like *'I'll Bet You'* were revolutionary: the approach to the music, the sensibility of the lyrics, the whole sonic dimension, right down to the sound of [drummer *Tiki Fulwood's*] snare drum. A lot of people didn't catch up with that shit for 10 more years."

One of George's favorite groups is *Cream*. They were a 60's trio of musicians from London, England, their line-up featured: *Jack Bruce*, bassist and singer, guitarist /singer *Eric Clapton* and drummer *Ginger Baker*. They were influenced by traditional and modern blues. Some of their biggest hits include *"Sunshine of Your Love"* a #5 hit in 1967 and *"White Room"*, #6 in 1968. Their niche style was a mix of blues/psychedelic rock. They also received stand-out recognition for their musicianship, especially their guitar driven tracks. *Cream* is considered one of the very first super rock groups. They are inducted in the *Rock and Roll Hall of Fame*.

The whole social turmoil that defined the 1960's was abstract to George and the band. They were so busy living the music, and the drug culture that although they were aware of what was happening in *Vietnam* or the *Martin Luther King* assassination, they could not grasp the incident or why it had to happen. George had settled into a new personal life in Canada with a former waitress named Elizabeth Bishop. He and Liz had a baby daughter named Barbarella and he was also a father figure to Liz's two children from a previous marriage. He was on the road a lot of the time. He stated, "Vietnam was an abstraction until it started to happen to specific people I knew, and even then, it was incomprehensible: young Americans being cut down in a distant land for reasons no one could adequately explain. Other events were equally abstract, even when they were thuddingly specific. When Martin Luther King Jr. was killed in Memphis, we were on the road. I don't know where, to be honest. Could have been Akron, Ohio. Could have been Ann Arbor, Michigan. All I know for sure is that I was backstage, tripping so hard that when a head poked around the door to tell me the news, I couldn't conceive of it".

Music became less a romantic way of getting women and more of a freedom to express a message of societal commentary, ideas and solutions. Drugs allowed artists to free their thinking for a while, but there would be serious consequences for their habits down the road. In real time, their drug of choice, LSD- acid, cleaned George and the guys and gals out. They spent many intimate times on the bathroom toilet due to it.

When George started his music journey in the fifties and into the sixties, an artist could create their music and stage presence. Those early years of beginning with black music label and moguls, like, *Golden World, Revilot, Invictus Westbound and later Casablanca* allowed him to develop his persona, musicians and sound. Because George developed personal and business partnerships with some key players, his reputation was well known to later label owners and he was able to gain their trust to evolve *Parliament* and *Funkadelic* into hit makers and live concert success.

10
Merging *Adelic* With Funk. The Beginning

The growth of *Funkadelic* came from the *Parliament* members and people that passed through George's *Silk Palace* barbershop. George was connecting with younger artists and living the lifestyle of many psychedelic-rock musicians of the day. In an interview in Michigan Music with P.T. Quinn in 2000, George says, "Why not the funk? I don't know no reason why not. Well, we were too late and too old to be Temptations. We were slick in our younger days, but by the time we got a hit record with *I Wanna Testify*, the *Cream, Led Zeppelin,* and *Jimi Hendrix* were comin' over with all of that funky rock & roll stuff…so even though I loved Motown all the while we were doing it, we missed the boat on being cool. We were just a little bit too old by the time we got our hit record *Testify* to be you know…. wooing little girls. I know one thing, characters don't get old. *Bugs Bunny, Woody Woodpecker,* and *Porky Pig* don't get old. We became *The Parli-Funkadelic-ment Thang*. Funkin' up things. Then we had our own space, we weren't fast rock & roll or slow blues. We had that mid-tempo music, that nasty music. So that's where some of my ideas for funk came from."

Young energy and ideas happened with *Billy "Bass" Nelson* who was a teenager that would hang out at the Silk Palace. Billy was the first member to join *Funkadelic*. He learned some guitar and helped George with lyrics. He also helped coin the name Funkadelic. Nelson was a prominent contributor to the first three *Funkadelic* albums, *Funkadelic* (1970), *Free Your Mind…and Your Ass Will Follow* (1970), and *Maggot Brain (1971).* Nelson left the group in late 1971 after a financial dispute with *George Clinton*. He was one of the first members to leave. This theme would be a major problem that would shadow Clinton in the late 1970s and early eighties. Another key member was *Eddie Hazel*, he joined George Clinton's music family in 1967 when he was only 17 years old. It took some convincing Hazel's mother that this new work opportunity was a good move for him.

Hazel was the guitar visionary of George Clinton's *Parliament-Funkadelic* empire. Born in Brooklyn in 1950, Hazel grew up in Plainfield, New Jersey, where he joined up with Clinton's funkateers. Hazel's 10-minute acid-rock emotional guitar solo made *Maggot Brain* the stand out title track on *Funkadelic*'s 1971 album. Clinton asked Hazel to imagine the saddest moment possible - his mother's death. *Maggot Brain* became a landmark of Hazel's artistry, he is considered by *Rolling Stone Magazine* to be one of the 100 Greatest Guitarists of All Time. Other tracks he can be heard on are: *I'll Bet You, Music for My Mother* and *Standing on the Verge on Getting It On*. Eddie also worked with the *Temptations* in the mid 70's, *Chairman of the Board*, and many other artists. *Eddie Hazel* died in 1992.

Between the years 1968 thru 1974 *Funkadelic* would build its band members and *Parliament* would evolve by gaining new young members as the music became less traditional vocal R&B and more blended with music and vocal styles of funk, jazz, pop and blues. *Parliament* evolved with psychedelic guitar, signature bass grooves, and wicked sound effects. *Funkadelic's* music vibe was more rock and funk grooves. Clinton became more inspired to be open at looking for ways to re-imagine his music compositions. Both groups were known for not only their artistic album covers, elaborate costumes or lack of clothes, but also for their theatrical stage shows. The whole package was an experience.

I recall when I left a little town in North Carolina,
I tried to escape this music I said it was for the old country folks
I went to New York, got slick, got my hair laid [laughs]
I was cool [more laughter]
I was cool
But I had no groove

Mommy, What's a Funkadelic?

On February 16, 1970, *Janus Records* which distributed the Westbound label introduced *Funkadelic* to the New York Press. The group gave a concert at the club *Ungano's* before disc jockeys and the media. *The Chess Record Company* was at one time a powerful label for black music artists in the classic genre of blues and soul, but by the 1970's was on a downward spiral with the company being sold to *Janus Records*. Founders Leonard and Phil Chess sold the company in 1969 for 6.9 million dollars. Leonard died in 1969 and his brother Phil and son Marshall left the company. After a decade of lukewarm releases, Janus Records vanished in 1979.

Multifarious Funk

The debut album release by *Parliament* in July 1970 was an album called *Osmium*. The album has a psychedelic *Funkadelic* soul sound. The group was moving away from their earlier R&B-inspired Parliament music and was released on *Invictus Records* in Detroit. It was a label started by music hit makers *Brian Holland, Lamont Dozier* and *Eddie Holland* after they left Motown in 1968. They had been *Motown*'s hit writers and producers on hundreds of songs on the label from 1962 thru 1967. *Osmium* was produced by Jeff Bowen and English folk singer Ruth Copeland. This album highlights the five original *Parliaments* singers. As this was the first album, the group was still re-inventing their sound. Some say it sounded more *Funkadelic* than *Parliament*.

I once had life, or rather
Life had me
I was one among many
Or at least I seemed to be
Well, I read an old quotation in a book yesterday
Said 'Gonna reap what you sow
The debts you make you have to pay
Can you get to that?" Lyrics to - *Can You Get to That?*

Billboard Magazine review read: 'something different and that's a good sign'.

The Parliaments joined their *Funkadelic* backing band on this album, The *Parliaments, Clarence "Fuzzy" Haskins,* was first tenor of the group. Original Parliament members *Calvin Simon* was first tenor vocalist and percussion player. Other original members from George's Silk Palace days are *"Shady Grady" Thomas,* baritone, *Clarence "Fuzzy" Haskins,* second tenor of the group and *Ray "Stingray" Davis* the original bass singer of the *Parliaments.*

Stingray's stand-out vocals on hits like *Tear the Roof off the Sucker (Give Up the Funk) and "Atomic Dog" are classic.* His distinctive voice can be heard on *Zapp's* hit, *I Can Make You Dance.* Davis also was a member of the *Temptations in the 1990's, t*aking over for their original bass singer *Melvin Franklin.* Ray was diagnosed with cancer in 1995 and left the *Temptations.* In spite of this, he toured with the *Parliaments'* original members for years. Ray passed away in 2005.

This debut album has been renamed in recent decades, alternative album names are *"Rhenium" and "First Thangs".* With these re-issued albums, some songs may not be included on the original debut album that may appear on these compilations. In addition, session musicians like *Bernie Worrell,* and *Gary Shider,* along with other band members may be on these albums.

The original *Funkadelic* band was equally amazing. They include *Ramon "Tiki" Fulwood,* vocalist and the original drummer for *Funkadelic.* Before P-Funk Fulwood had been the house drummer for Philadelphia's *Uptown Theatre.* He originally quit the band in 1971, but reappeared on several *Parliament-Funkadelic albums over the years.* He died in 1979.

Lucius "Tawl Ross was the rhythm guitarist on *Funkadelic's* first three albums. He left the band in 1971, but from time to time he would join the group in the studio on some of their gold and platinum albums. Mickey Atkins was the original keyboard player for *Funkadelic*. He was replaced officially by Bernie Worrell in the early 1970's. Billy "Bass" Nelson is the original bass guitarist for *Funkadelic*, Eddie Hazel was friends with Billy "Bass Nelson."

"The Kingdom of Heaven is Within.

Open You Funky Mind and You Can Fly." - *Free Your Mind*

The second studio album by *Funkadelic* is *"Free Your Mind…and Your Ass Will Follow."* It was released in July 1970 by Westbound Records. *Westbound Records* was founded in Detroit by *Armen Boladian* in 1970. Armen was a record producer. Under his time at *Westbound* the label had success with *Funkadelic* and early recordings by the *Ohio Players and the Detroit Emeralds*.

George has stated that he and the band wanted to see if they could make a whole album "while tripping on acid." Critics at the time thought this album to be weird and too much of a mixed message. But George was challenging his listeners to think for themselves. It seemed that the sixties message of love and freedom, togetherness and peace was now being stopped by new corporate rules of conforming any innovation or individualism. Think for yourself!

George says: "Everyone was on acid – the audience, everyone – so it didn't matter. Acid ain't the same as before anyway. It's full of poison now that money and corporations are involved. I never had a bad trip on the acid in the 60s, only when they started putting angel dust and shit in it. Even street drugs are done by pharmaceutical companies now. I wouldn't trust no drugs these days."

But consumers have grown to love this eclectic contradiction of Christianity, Spirituality and space funk/rock with bible verses and spoken catchphrases. The *Free Your Mind* album featured a woman with hand extended toward the sky, but the cover inside sleeve showed the woman nude. Motown great *Martha Reeves* appears on this album but is uncredited. Vocalist *Thelma Hopkins and Joyce Vincent of Dawn* also appear on a single called *Friday Night, August 14th*.

Bass and percussion was very dominant in the *Funkadelic* sound George says, "Doo-Wop had a bass voice and guitar, but as far as a bass instrument, it was James Jameson and them at Motown who put the funk IN. It was so sophisticated it probably got past a lot of people. They did it in unison with vibes and piano. *The Four Tops* and everything. You couldn't get away from it, they had bottom on that stuff. It used to be upright bass, and that was slick, but I put the electric bass all the way on top. I made the drums and bass the loudest thing on our records. You can almost run your hand across the vinyl and feel a lump in it. I tried to make the needle jump up off the record. Yeah, we accentuated the bass. Every time we hit on something that was truly funky, we went overboard with it. Free your mind your ass will follow…we just went totally NUTS! I mean it was the day of the drugs but it wasn't as much as the record indicated. Even though the drugs may have given us the nerve to do it, we weren't as f--ked up as we sounded. We were out there though; you know what I'm saying? But that was pretty much normal at that time. Everybody was experiencing a new vibe 'cause that was the thing that stopped the (Vietnam) war. Tune in, turn on, and drop out. Till the war dropped out it was what everybody did. But the minute it became for sale…(pauses) it was over too. When Woodstock happened, drug culture was over, I mean as a positive thing. It was business after that. It was "do you want to buy a lid?" And when it becomes that, you got to be careful."

In 1970, *Funkadelic* made a rare TV appearance on the teen music dance and variety show called *UpBeat* taped in Cleveland Ohio at ABC-TV affiliate WEWS-TV 5. The host was Don Webster.

They sang, *I Got A Thang*. All members were decked out in individual outfits: Indian, Warlock, Hippie, and other personas. They played their psychedelic track and teen-heart throb and former *Shindig* regular *Bobby Sherman* followed them singing his new hit! What a unique contrast of music styles!

Multifarious Funk

The album *Maggot Brain* dropped in 1971, it was recorded at Universal Sound Studios in Detroit. The single has become quite famous because of a 10-minute solo by guitarist Eddie Hazel. The lyrics to the song speak of the mind.

"I have tasted the maggots in the mind of the universe
I was not offended for I knew I had to rise above it all"

The famous song *Can You Get to That*, had been re-written and renamed on this album, it had been a *Parliament* song called *"Where You Been Grown"* a break-up song. The *Funkadelic* version is more a reflective song about life's lessons and karma. George said that engineers did not want their names on the album.

In Cleveland Ohio at WMMS a tradition of playing *"Maggot Brain"* every Sunday Morning at 1:30 AM., was started by *Bill "B.L.F. Bash" Freeman* in 1976. It continues today on WNCX with *Mr. Classic* host of *The Saturday Night Live House party*, at ten minutes before mid-night.

10 Merging Adelic With Funk. The Beginning

Multifarious Funk

11
Eclectic Imaging

Funkadelic album covers would be a bit surprising. On *Maggot Brain* a *sistah* is pictured with her head sticking out of the earth, even liner notes that were lifted from a Scientology spin-off called the *Church of Final Judgment*. But they really did not show the band's personality. Outside of t-shirts, posters, and concerts, the marketing for funk music groups was just really beginning and most of that responsibility fell on the group.

Funkadelic toured The United Kingdom in the spring of 1971. They were set to play the famed *Royal Albert Hall* May 12th, however when a representative Miss Marion Herold of *Albert Hall* heard the lyrics to their music *Free Your Mind………and Your Ass Will Follow*, the show was canceled! She said, "There are just some bookings I do not like to take, I don' think I can say more than that."

In the Summer of June 1971 in New York, the *Chess Family of record labels* held a distributor sale convention for the *Chess, Janus,* and

Westbound Records. This convention was attended by representatives in 22 cities. Artists like: *Etta James, Moms Mabley, Muddy Water, Pigmeat Markham, Rotary Connection* and *Funkadelic* were being marketed through special promotion campaigns to people in the radio and record industry. Late that summer, the band played Gaslight Au Go-Go in New York on September 15th and 16th. They then headed to the West Coast for about a month from September 21st to October 14th and lastly to South Africa November 14th thru December 26th.

11   Eclectic Imaging

In 1973, *Funkadelic*'s fifth album called *Cosmic Slop* shipped. Although this album was not commercially successful, it marked a beginning of a new relationship that would last through the millennium. The artwork and liner notes were created by a young artist named Pedro Bell. His illustrations explained the album's songs to fans and brought them into the band's mythology. According to Pedro "I dropped P-Funk a hand-designed envelope duplicating a dollar bill with the address where the serial number is supposed to go."

Pedro was an untrained artist who had a knack of illustrating *Funkadelic's* growing vision and super hero characters. While working for George, Pedro kept his day jobs as a postal worker and security guard. Clinton asked him to do the artwork for his 1973 album *Cosmic Slop* and his work impacted the black art world. He helped define the *P-Funk* Empire in terms of marketing as his artwork became posters of the musical experience for fans. His work would continue not only for *Funkadelic* albums but also for George's later solo albums.

Should there be some who would choose to ignore this maladroided message of doom, I further proclaim it to be the right of the noble followers of FUNKADELIA to counteract the inane, infantile antics of those pimpatory, sapless stooges and exploitive ecdysiasts of evil. FUNKADELIA IS UPON THEE!"

Cosmic Slop Liner Notes

Multifarious Funk

In June 1973, *Funkadelic* was on a concert line-up with headliners Rare Earth, Buddy Miles and Mandrill at Robert F. Kennedy Memorial Stadium in Washington, D.C. The mostly black crowd was estimated at about 60,000 in attendance. Although Rare Earth was a white band, their manager Ron Strassner cited that the other acts on the bill were also responsible for that huge turnout.

The fourth album by *Funkadelic* called *American Eats Its Young*, introduced a group of new musicians who would make up the backbone of *Parliament-Funkadelic's* success. It was a *Westbound Records* album release in 1972. The musicians to first make their appearance with the troupe were: *Bootsy Collins, Catfish Collins, Chicken Gunnels, Rob McCollough and Kash Waddy,* also, Guitarist *Garry Shider* and bassist *Cordell Mosson* - Plainfield, New, Jersey natives that had formed *a band called United Soul*. They knew George from their days at *the Silk Palace*. Both are also on this album. This was a double LP recorded in Toronto Canada, and the United Kingdom.

The song *"Everybody is Going to Make It This Time"* featured one of George's favorite English drummers *Ginger Baker*. He was an original founder of one of George's favorite rock bands - *Cream*.

The album was the first to debut the *Funkadelic* band logo on the cover. It also contained a poster by artist Cathy Abel.

George was very impressed with a young William "Bootsy" Collins when they had briefly met a few years earlier. Mallia Franklin, future member of the P-Funk tribe suggested George look at him. He and his older brother Phelps "Catfish" Collins who played rhythm guitar had been with James Brown during their tenure in the J.B.'s. They recorded classic hits: *Super Bad, (I Feel Like Being A) Sex Machine, Soul Power and Give It Up or Turn it a Loose.*

George explained his idea of *Funkadelic's* continued growth and his attitude in keeping the groups sound fresh by switching things up. He said: "By that point, the widening group of musicians around us also included Garry Shider and Boogie Mosson, from United Soul, both of whom would be instrumental to our growth over the coming decade. *Funkadelic* had always been a hybrid of other things. First the original Parliaments and the psychedelic rock that was happening all around it, and the second wave of musicians reaffirmed my belief in the way to grow. Absorb youth and you will be absorbed by youth. Take on new influences without fear and you need not fear what is new. Change the people around you by changing the people around you"."

The *Parliament- Funkadelic* sound would become famous, due to George cultivating relationships with young and innovative musicians. *Bernie Worrell* would prove to be another invaluable member. Although George knew him at age 14 before he went to college, Bernie Worrell, who officially joined *Funkadelic* after the release of their first album made his innovative use of synthesizers very influential, particularly his pioneering use of a deep, heavy Moog synthesizer sound to reinforce the bass line.

Bernie Worrell was a classically trained musician from Julliard and the New England Conservatory of Music. His mother resented his interest in joining the group. A young music prodigy, Bernie played the Apollo Theatre with singer *Maxine Brown* and with the group *Chubby and the Turnpikes*. Their name was changed to *Tavares* in the 1970's and the group had several top 10 R & B hits like *Heaven Must Be Missing an Angel* and *Remember*. *The Turnpike's* drummer was *Joey Kramer*, later of the rock group *Aerosmith*. Worrell left the band in 1981. In fact, George was an admirer of Joey's rhythmic grooves with *Aerosmith* and compares the band's influence on 1970's rock pioneer group *Led Zeppelin*.

Bernie would later go on to produce *The Talking Heads*. He contributed to *Give Up the Funk (Tear the Roof Off the Sucker)* from the *Mothership Connection* album and *Aqua Boogie from the Motor Booty Affair*. Worrell left the band in 1981, but continued to contribute to *P-Funk* studio albums and occasionally appeared live with *Parliament-Funkadelic* as a special guest. In 2015, Worrell appeared in the movie *Ricki and the Flash* as the keyboard player in *Meryl Streep's* band.

An advertisement for this Westbound Records album announced that it was inspired by teachings from *The Process----Church of the Final Judgment*.

> Funk transcends the ceremony and ritual of religion
> and goes right to the core: love for your enemies,
> truth and revolution.

Revolution of the heart and mind.
And it gets across in the music that's not easily forgotten.
"America Eats Its Young".
Sometimes you have to lose your mind to gain your soul.
It was available on 8 Track Stereo Cartridges and Cassettes!!

Standing on the Verge of Getting it On

"As it is written henceforth…. that on the Eight Day,

The Cosmic Strumpet of MOTHER NATURE was

spawned to envelop this Third Planet in

FUNKACIDAL VIBRATIONS, And She birthed

Apostles, Ra, Hendrix, Stone & Clinton to preserve

all funkiness of man into eternity…"

(Wet Debauchery" liner notes, *Standing on the Verge of getting It On*, (1974)

Another unique work on *Westbound Records* was the 1974 album *Standing on the Verge of Getting It On. Eddie Hazel* co-wrote the songs on this album with George, but credited them under his mother Grace Cook. The lyrics generally take a backseat to the music and Eddie's guitar work and it is considered one of the most popular *Funkadelic* albums ever among fans. The album artwork by *Pedro Bell* featured monsters, aliens and a kingdom of other worldly creatures, and is truly a storybook attraction.

In the millennium, this song still lives on and was brought to new audiences by way of the *Tonight Show with Jimmy Fallon.* In 2014, *The Red Hot Chili Peppers* along with the show house band *The Roots* performed *Standing on the Verge of Getting It On. On that episode,* the Peppers' drummer Chad Smith and look-a-like Hollywood actor *Will Ferrell* were in a drum battle. *Funkadelic* toured without Eddie for this album. It was on tour in Cleveland, Ohio that George discovered a seventeen-year-old that could play Eddie Hazel's famous guitar solo on the single *Maggot Brain* note for note, he was *Michael Hampton*. Impressed with his talent and seeing his potential as a permanent band member, George met with his folks to see if he could tour with the group. With their ok, he became a permanent band member. Press Releases and Marketing for the album included an article in 1974 in *Blues and Soul Magazine* entitled *Funkadelic and Parliament - On the Verge of Getting It on Again*.

12
Charting Fresh Territory

Within the same month, George revived his Parliament genre on a new label with an old acquaintance who was starting his own record label. This next musical move would land George and his troupe the most commercial success of their careers. *Neil Bogart* was an up and coming music mogul in the making when George was in Detroit in the late 60's. Bogart was born in New York City, and grew up in the housing projects of Brooklyn. He was a singer in the 1960's on cruise ships. He also had a minor regional hit called *Bobby* under the stage name *Neil Scott*. He would later work for *Cashbox Magazine*; rising to promotional director for MGM records. At age 24, he became the youngest record executive to run *Cameo-Parkway Records* in Michigan.

One of his success moves was acquiring a composition from the group *Question Mark and the Mysterians.* The group was from Saginaw, Michigan. Lead singer *Rudy Martinez* singing under the stage name "*? Mark*" wrote a poem called *Too Many Tear Drops;* it was turned into a song entitled *69 Tears*. When Neil heard the song, he suggested it be renamed *96 Tears*. It became a regional hit after being promoted on CKLW in Windsor, Ontario. The hit caught Neil's attention and after he purchased the rights to the song, he promoted the hit and the band nationally. They appeared in pop music shows like *American Bandstand, Where the Action Is* and national tours with major pop bands of the day like the *Beach Boys and The Mama's and the Papa's. 96 Tears* became a million-disc seller in the fall of 1966. Before *Cameo-Parkway Records* was shut down by the government for stock fraud in 1968, Bogart became an executive at *Buddha Records*. He became a key player in the promotion of bubblegum pop music during his time working at *Cameo-Parkway and Buddha*. At *Buddha*, there were also independent labels for artists, such as the label Curtom for *Super Fly*, Curtis Mayfield's #8 hit in 1972; *Bill Withers was on the* Sussex *label*, he scored the hit *Use Me* in 1972; *and Honey Cone* hit #1 with *"Want Ads in* 1971 on the Hot Wax label.

On the national charts the label also had hits like *Green Tamborine by the Lemon Pipers*, a #1 hit in 1968; 1-*2-3- Red Light* by the 1910 Fruitgum *Company* in 1968. *Brother Louie* by T*he Stories* hit #1 in 1973; *Laydown* by vocalist *Melaine* rose to #7 in 1970; *O-o-h Child* by *The Five Stairsteps* was #8 on the Billboard charts in 1970; *Oh Happy Day* by *The Edwin Hawkins Singers* hit #4 in 1969. After they left *Motown*, The *Isley Brothers* had a mega Billboard ranked #2 hit with *It's Your Thing*, in 1969. This hit garnered them a *Grammy Award* in 1970 and the first former *Motown* group to do so. The impressive list goes on. Neil was responsible in helping develop a variety of music artists, genres and the label to national success.

Neil founded the independent label, *Casablanca Records*, in 1973. One of the first artists to sign with him was the rock group *KISS*, the other was *Parliament*. George knew Neil from Detroit and felt Neil would be on board with the re-introduction of *Parliament*. He was young, open to new ideas, and helped to support his artists in brand promotion. Their debut album on *Casablanca*, *Up For the Down Stroke* and single *Up For the Down Stroke* became the group's first top #10 hit. *Bootsy Collins* also returned to the group as a musician and was a writer on the title cut.

Collins and his band the *House Guests* included his brother *Phelps "Catfish" Collins, Rufus Allen, Clayton "Chicken" Gunnels, Frankie Waddy, Ronnie Greenaway and Robert McCullough*. Singles released by the *House Guests* include: *What So Never the Dance"* and others on the *House Guest label*. In addition, ex-Madhouse singer-drummer *Gary "Mudbone" Cooper* joined *Parliament/Funkadelic*.

"Although it was a major success, George was too absorbed in creating new music, the groups commercial popularity was a two-edged sword. He says "success brought more money in the short term, which increased the number of hangers-on and improved the quality of drugs. But even that wasn't as drastic as it was with some other bands, largely because when we made money, we spent it on new sessions, new equipment and tour props. The arrangement seemed to work for everyone. Neil never minded that we were blowing up as *Funkadelic*. I would let him come in and listen to the tracks, and if there was one he felt strongly about keeping with *Parliament*, I'd Let it go that way."

Marketing for this album included: film footage of George in platforms and Funkenstein outfit and boom box. He is jamming to the music in the streets with other fans making their way to the *Record Connection* store.

P-Funk attracted the best and brightest talent. But with that exposure, it brought issues with teens and their introduction to excess sex, drugs and accountability. To help George, they employed a cousin of Mike's named Lodge. George says "Tiki was the furthest out on the ledge. He would drop acid with Mike, and as soon as they were high, he would steal Mike's money or even his clothes. Now that's high"!

Chocolate Devotees

"They still call it the White House, but that's a temporary condition," Chocolate City

Chocolate City was the third album, released on Casablanca Records in 1975. It was done as a tribute to Washington, D.C. and sold a bit over 150,000 there alone. The single *'Chocolate City"* was a bit prophetic in its lyrics. Its album image included *The White House, Lincoln, Washington Monument and The Lincoln Memorial* as a chocolate medallion on the front cover. Its lyrics promoted black pride. George also would mention other cities with a black majority population in the song. His presidential cabinet included popular black entertainers of the day like *Muhammad Ali* as the President; *Reverend Ike* as Secretary of Treasury; *Stevie Wonder* as Secretary of Fine Arts; *Richard Pryor* as Minster of Education and *Aretha Franklin* as The First Lady.

The single *'Chocolate City"* was a bit prophetic in its lyrics. The United States Department of Education was not established until the Carter Administration in 1979. On this album guitarist *Prakash John* and the *Brecker Brothers, Randy* and *Michael* join the group. It is also the first appearance by vocalist *Glen Goins*. He was an important contributor to the band until 1978 when he left and formed his own band, *Quazar* with *Jerome "Bigfoot" Brailey*. Goins was known for his gospel-influenced vocal style. Glen died from Hodgkin's lymphoma at age 24.

Let's Take It to The Stage album was released in 1975. The stand out song on this album is "*Get Off Your Ass and Jam."* It was the breakout chant that Parliament needed and got back from their audience at their live concerts. Ned Raggett reviewed the song as one that "kicks in with one bad-ass drum roll and then scorches the damn place down".

This contagious chant was so popular that the 1975 movie *Rocky Horror Picture Show*, after the *Time Warp* ended, has a line *"Shit! Goddamn it! Get off your ass and slam it Janet"*

13
60's 70's Space, Cosmic Influence and George

Starting after the World War II, some findings of the U.S. Government started dominating the world news. Hollywood began to make movies and attempted to explore outer space. In the early 1950's movies of outer space, the planet beings, were portrayed as aliens with unbelievably exaggerated looks by most cultural standards. New worlds or galaxies were the subjects of literature. The other world beings were portrayed as evil, scary and ready to annihilate earthlings. In the 1960's aliens were comical, smarter than us, supernatural and a bit more human like. They broadcast in our living rooms on top 10 TV series like: *The Twilight Zone, My Favorite Martian, Man from Atlantis, Lost in Space,* and *The Jetsons*. The race to put a man in space happened first in the late 1950's by the Russians; and in America, *President Kennedy* vowed to put a man in space under the *Kennedy Administration* in 1962, and on the moon in 1969.

In the media, aliens could be friendly. Or they could be seductive or zombie creeps that could scare the *sh*t* out of you. In the 1970's, the supernatural was newsworthy. Whether it was media about clones, news about mysterious crop circles or Area 51. Even popular movies like *"Close Encounters of the Third Kind", "Star Wars"* and the TV shows like *"Battle Star Galactica"* engaged audiences worldwide. George was a *"Star Trek"* fan and loves the movie *"Star Wars"* and "other world" media themes.

George and the guys were invited to a party for the premiere of Steven Spielberg's movie "*Close Encounters of the Third Kind*" in 1977. Although the excitement of seeing the spaceship and the Dolby four-track stereo sound was amazing, he left the event with questions, "I wanted space movies to answer where our world came from. Did aliens come down to help the Egyptians build the Pyramids? Were they going to come back later whether or not we had our thumbs up to hitch a ride?"

In the millennium, these shows and movies are cult classics that can be seen in re-runs today, loved by five generations and growing. There are even sci-fi conventions where fans can meet their favorite actor or alien from these shows. With the exception of actress Nichelle Nichols who portrayed Lieutenant Nyota Uhura in the original *Star Trek* TV series there were no other black folk in outer space and clearly no *black brothas*. That is, until George Clinton's intergalactic alter egos.

The music of *Funkadelic* in the early 70's took on a soulful fusion of rock- funk, jazz mixed with a message of peace, spirituality and social awakening to changes in humanity. Songs like *Funk Dollar Bill* and albums like *Free Your Mind..........* and *Maggot Brain* explore the uncool effects of mind conformity, commercialism and materialism. The return of *Parliament* in 1975 saw a more cosmic look at divinity. The word FUNK is the source of life as described in the song *P-Funk -Who Wants to Get Funked Up* from the album *Mothership Connection*. The song was written by George, Bootsy and Bernie Worrell.

In the live show's clips of the *P-Funk Tour*, *Parliament* member *Glen Goins'* gospel blues vocals can be heard calling in the *Mothership*, to land on the stage for the *P-Funk* opera. Glen Goins was an extraordinary vocalist. He did back-up vocals for soul vocalist Bobby Womack. In fact, Glen was so good a singer that Bobby fired him and told Glen to get his own gigs!

George's vision of the *Mothership* meant a way for the minds of black people to be liberated from troubles, racism and stresses of the world. It was a monument to black people. In the live shows featuring The *Mothership*, Bernie Walden, a roadie for *P-Funk* said, "The smoke was so thick it billowed with carbon dioxide that people in the front row were passing out." Bernie half humorously called the shows organized mayhem. So, there it was, Sci-Funk & FUN!!

The *Parliament* album *Mothership Connection* released in 1975 on Casablanca Records, marked a major turning point for the group. The million selling hit *Tear the Roof of the Sucker* became *Parliament's* first Gold disc. The single also had another song *P- Funk (Wants to Get Funked up) on the B –side*. It became *Parliament's* first album to be certified gold and later platinum The Library of Congress added the album to the National Recording Registry in 2011, declaring "the album has had an enormous influence on jazz, rock and dance music." *Rolling Stone Magazine* said it was the bomb,' as Clinton succinctly put it before anyone else."

Jerome "Bigfoot" Brailey was the most prominent drummer in the *Parliament-Funkadelic* collective during their period of greatest success in the mid-to late 1970s. He started as the drummer with the Howard University based group the *Unifics*. Some of their music was arranged by a young student named *Donny Hathaway*. Then he recorded with the *Five Stairsteps* on their classic hit *O-o-h Child"* in 1971. He also performed with *The Chamber Brothers*. He and *Glen Goins* left the *P-Funk* groups in 1978. Both went on to form *Quazar* till Goins' death in 1978, and afterwards, Brailey started his group *Mutiny*. Jerome co-wrote *Tear the Roof Off the Sucker* and *Give Up the Funk* with George and Bootsy in 1975.

In the September 1976, *Westbound* finally realized the rising popularity of *Funkadelic*. The label decided to use outtakes of a recording session that George had given to them as part of a contractual agreement. The last album with *Westbound* was *Tales of Kidd Funkadelic*. Young guitarist Michael Hampton's nickname was *Kidd Funkadelic*.

The band left the label for Warner Brothers Records and now had their new album ready to be released. It was called *Hardcore Jollies* and was released October of 1976. This album features standout performances by Eddie Hazel. This would be the last *Funkadelic* album to include the original *Parliaments*: Fuzzy Haskins, Calvin Simon and Grady Thomas. The album is dedicated to "the guitar players of the world."

A *Funkadelic Pre- Sale!!* advertisement for the Warner Brothers' album *Hardcore Jollies* states: By the time the biggest tour in the history of black music ends, close to 2 million customers will have been pre-sold on the biggest Funkadelic album in history. - Billboard Nov 13, 1976

From late October at Louisiana State University in Baton Rouge through the end of December in Atlanta, Georgia on New Year's Eve 1976, *Parliament-Funkadelic*'s Earth Tour A.D ended with *33* cities on its schedule!

"Funk upon a time, in the days of the Funkapuss, the concept of specially designed Afro-nauts capable of funkatizing galaxies, was first laid on Man Child, but was later repossessed and placed among the secrets of the pyramids, until a more positive attitude towards this most sacred phenomenon, Clone Funk, could be acquired. There in these terrestrial projects it would wait along with its co-inhabitants, the Kings and Pharaohs, like sleeping beauties, for the kiss that would release them to multiply in the image of the Chosen One, Dr. Funkenstein. And funk is its own reward. May I frighten you?"

("Prelude," *The Clones of Dr. Funkenstein* (1976)

Multifarious Funk

14
Original P Checked Out

"The mere fact of surviving in this industry is a huge victory. But survivors forget that the alternative is annihilation."

—George Clinton

There were three members of the original Parliament that left the organization in 1977. Clarence "Fuzzy" Haskins, Grady Simon and Calvin decide to move on. They had helped start the young members of the group from Plainfield in the early seventies like *Billy Nelson, Ramon "Tiki" Fulwood, Bernie Worrell, and Eddie Hazel* grow and mature. But the *P-Funk* organization expansion started in 1974 kept growing with a new record label management/advisers, new musicians and vocalists, break-out artists, and most likely they felt less featured vocal work for them.

George reflects: "People don't have a clear idea of what they can and can't do as artists. I knew my limits. I knew what I couldn't do, I couldn't play an instrument. I couldn't sing as well as some and I couldn't arrange as well as some others. But I could see the whole picture from altitude, and that let me land the planes"

The younger band members helped to inspire the more seasoned musicians. George also evolved his cosmic visions for the groups. With most of the original *Parliament* leaving as the *Parliament-Funkadelic* groups were growing into big success, the only member to remain was bass singer *Ray Davis*. He became a group member of the *Parliaments* in 1961. Ray stayed with George till about 1984.

The Original P reorganized and toured with their own band. They also broke with the profanity in their music and stage act, *Fuzzy Haskins* became an ordained minister. The original singers kept their love of vocal harmonies in their music act as well as including some early *Funkadelic* singles like *Maggot Brain* and *Can You Get to That?* in their live shows. Original P also began recording new material in the 1980's.

No other major artist during that decade was more prolific than Clinton, who, beginning in 1970, recorded 19 studio albums (11 by Funkadelic, eight by Parliament, a number of them undisputed classics). P-Funk concerts became legend. On any given night, there might be upwards of 30 musicians onstage, black hippie freaks wearing turbans, top hats, sombreros, face paint, S&M gear, fencing masks, space-pimp platform shoes, prosthetic Pinocchio noses, dashikis, chaps, starry-lensed sunglasses and (in the case of guitarist Garry Shider) nothing but a diaper. Clinton himself emerged from a giant flying saucer. They called him Dr. Funkenstein.

Starchild

Well Alright!

Starchild. Citizens of the Universe
Recording Angels

We have returned to claim the Pyramids
partying on the Mothership

I am the Mothership Connections
Gettin down in 3-D...............

Lyrics *Starchild*

The Mothership Connection, or Starchild, the original name when it was released in 1975 as a single, has been revived for G-Funk fans thanks to artist, now producer, *Dr. Dre.* His 1992 single *Let Me Ride*, was a major crossover hit, it introduced a new generation to the original music of *Parliament.*

"Swing down, sweet chariot. Stop and let me ride."

Multifarious Funk

15
Takin' It to the Mothership

Parliament-Funkadelic had tours before, but not like this! The *P-Funk Earth* Tour was a carefully planned production with many rehearsals stage cues, lighting, props, choreography and songs to enhance the show. All forty musicians of the *P-Funk* rehearsed at Hanger E, Stewart Airport about 15 minutes outside Newburgh, New York and Maceo Parker oversaw the music arrangements. The band *Aerosmith* had retired their stage equipment in 1976, so it was available for George and crew. Jules Fisher designed and built the *Mothership*. He was a lighting designer who worked with Broadway, TV, Film and many Rock & Roll tour productions and won numerous Tony Awards for his work. Its cost was at least half a million dollars. The leather suits for George and the band were about $10,000 each.

The shows debut happened in October of 1976 at the Municipal Auditorium in New Orleans. In the beginning of the first show, the *Mothershi*p sailed above the heads of the audience. The band then went on to perform their show. It was during those shows that George felt that the ship overshadowed them. The *Mothership* entrance was a hard act to follow. So, after the show, he decided to have the *Mothership* as a finale of the show. He said, "It was so powerful-and such a perfect way to cap off the concert, with Glen calling the ship down-that it took your breath away."

George emphasized the young band members like *Glen Goins and Garry Shider.* Not only were they enigmatic but they also had the pulse of the young crowd. Glen took the crowd *to* church with his gospel vocals. The *Parliament* tour set included *Sly Stone* opening for them: *Bootsy Collins*, was becoming a break-out star from *P-Funk,* but at the time he was also still performing with the group. Because of his charisma, Bootsy could just stand on stage and the audience would go wild. And that is before he even sang a note! Finally, the *Parliament-Funkadelic* took to the stage singing their hits like:

Do That Stuff, Cosmic Slop, Night of the Thumpasaurus People, and more. In 1976, Bootsy also had his *Stretchin Out Tour* launching to support his album and singles *I'd Rather Be with You* and *Stretchin Out*. Both singles were top 30 hits on the R&B charts.

There were normal things that bothered George about the show like the issue of dropped cues, problems with the sound or lighting. But nothing stood out more than the *Mothership* hovering over the audience, it was throwing off sparks! What he wanted was his spaceship and he got it. But now with the show happening in real time, he saw questions of safety concerns for the audiences that paid their money to see the *P-Funk* live. He could see it was a liability if the ships equipment malfunctioned and it landed on his fans. After a couple dozen shows, the small ship was retired. During every night of the tour, the stage set, props, and equipment needed to be packed onto seven trucks. Each night, the live shows were a unique experience as all were not in large auditoriums. So, the ship could not work in many outdoor theaters, stadiums or many small concert halls.

And, many problems that were financial were beginning to surface for the band; one tour assistant's job was "to tell the musicians why they weren't getting paid." *The P-Funk* had the marketing and promotions in check, but the shows were losing a lot of money as time went on. The shows helped to build their brand and this also helped them to continue to get Neil's support so they could grow their acts and related projects, but still *The Parliament-Funkadelic Tour* was losing money.

Neil being a promotions genius hired a lieutenant of the air force to travel with the band. And the band got trips to NORAD-the North American Aerospace Defense Command in Colorado and a few *NASA* facilities too. Because of its elaborate stage presence, *The Mothership* became a celebrity.

Multifarious Funk

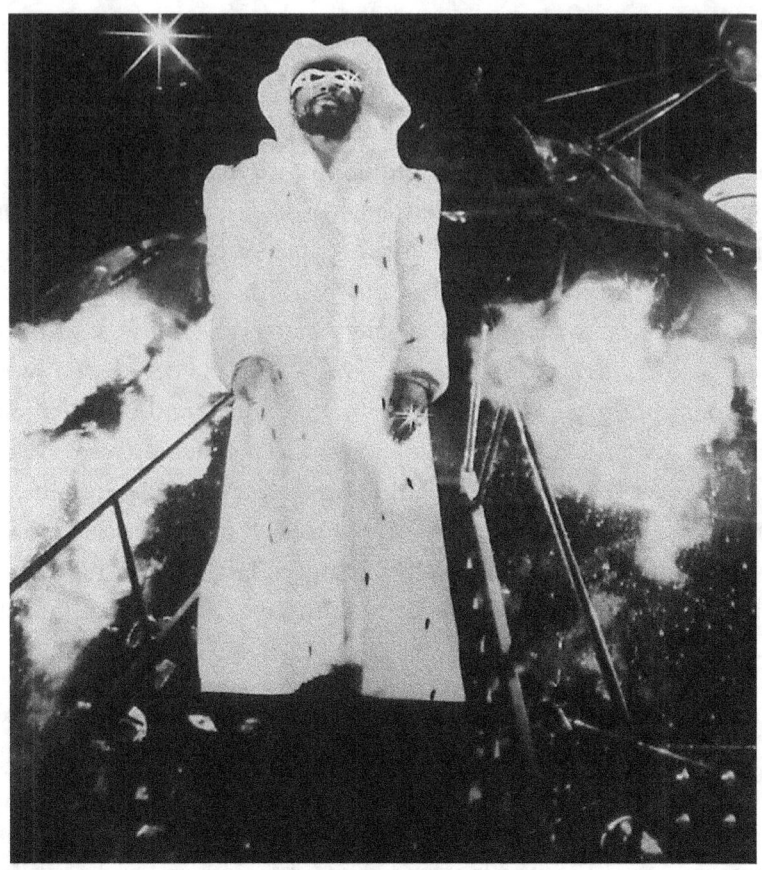

The funk opera was a hit that attracted people from all walks of life and many groups of faith. The album the *P-Funk Earth Tour* was recorded in January of 1977 at both the Los Angeles Forum and the Oakland Coliseum. It also included remakes of songs from other albums. Manager Cholly Bassoline said that 'You did not have to get high to be high at *P-Funk Shows*. The show could go on for hours."

The group always had crossover appeal. In June 1974, *Parliament-Funkadelic* tours with a few other acts on the bill at Kennedy Stadium were averaging about 80,000 in attendance. By the way, the other acts on the bill had no music on the current music charts at that time, so *P-Funk* fans made up most of that tour.

15   Takin' It to the Mothership

In 1976, their current area tours had more than 1 million people in attendance. *The P-Funk Earth Tour 1976-77 A.D.* which had dates in 75 U.S. cities, was considered to be the biggest tour by a black act as it rolled into Providence, Rhode Island's Civic Center. According to George, his fans, were smart and spent their money to see a quality show, not the bubble-gum fluff. It was not about being cute or a fad, it was about the music and the show. For nine months out of the year the P-Funk troupe toured the country.

George says, modestly, that the true creative father is comedian Richard Pryor, but that's blue funk. Clinton's own definition of funk is "the way blacks act when they are together," but the idea perhaps comes across better in one of his lyrics: *"Shake, goddamn / Get off your ass and jam."* Surprisingly, perhaps, Clinton's group was integrated, and, in a business more sexist than racist, two are women. P-Funk (as the Clinton musical conglomerate was known) had crossover appeal. Otherwise, it would never have sold one platinum and two gold records or launched a 100-city-tour of mostly 10,000-seat arenas.

Multifarious Funk

16
Agents of
Supergroovalisticprosifunkstication

Multifarious Funk

From the start, the *P-Funk* organization had their own unique way of promotion with their music, album covers, personas and more. But when they traveled to do radio promotions, they had a three-tiered approach: *Bootsy* would do an interview on one station, George would talk with another station in that town and *Funkadelic* would be at yet another. The DJ's promoting at their concerts ALL had to dress the theme of the show by wearing spacesuits. In addition, George's other ingenious idea, was to have the DJ's have their wives get promoter's licenses. He says "This was something I remembered from the mid-sixties, from when Armen took me around to stations in the Mid-west. If DJ's set their wives up as promoters, they didn't have to pay a deposit to a promoter. We didn't let them pay us less than a promoter would, but we didn't ask for more either. This empowered DJ's and made them more than happy to work with us."

In the seventies, race was an issue on many levels. With their new-found success came questions of who oversees the money? Who was selling the tickets? This challenge came from civil rights leader *Hosea Williams*. When he discovered that George and the group yearly made charitable contributions of twenty-five cents from each ticket to the *United Negro College Fund* from their large concerts, he backed off. In 1978, the group raised $18,000 for UNCF.

There was even protesting over Who was promoting the show? Believe it or not, *P-Funk* had people picketing their concert because they felt their operations were all black. Well, George had an integrated business duo, a white woman and black man, with a company called *Tiger Flower* out of Washington, D.C. to promote their concerts. George felt it best to defuse situations for a win-win outcome.

The funk genre was not even budgeted for like artists in Pop, Rock, R&B and Disco but most of those artists had mainstreamed their sound to fit into the Pop category. Rock groups got more money and English groups got great money. Although *Parliament* tried to define a black rock category, they were stuck with R&B. The black acts had very low budgets. Even with hugely successful *P-Funk* albums and singles that sold into gold and platinum status their budgets were low compared to rock acts. But, the *P-Funk* groups were breaking the traditional music genres down, converting old foes and their influence like their message of spirit and evolution was spawning..........New fans.

Multifarious Funk

17
R&B, Crossover vs. Real Funk

In the 1940's, the term Rhythm and Blues was coined as a friendly term for black music. According to George, music terms change with time. "Terminology for black music has undergone so many name changes as traditional blues, gospel, have been mixed with Swing, Jazz and other categories of music". In the 1950's, music terms were Race Music, Doo-Wop and Cross-Over. An interesting example of this is *Hank Ballard*'s mega hit "*The Twist*". It was on a label categorized as "Race Music". Philadelphia's music promoter Dick Clark got Ernest Evans to record the song, he even sounded similar to Hank. But Ernest aka *Chubby Checker*'s version became better known going to number #1 in 1961 and 1962. James Brown's band mixed elements of blues gospel, jazz, and funk.

In the 60's Motown hits were R&B Pop music, its base was the deep groove of bassist *James Jamerson* and the *Funk Brothers*, Motown's backing band. Only a few artists on their Soul labels were pushing for pure funk. Then there was R&B, Bubble-gum Rock and Psychedelic Rock of the 60's. In the 1970's, it was Disco, Pop, Rock, Punk, Quiet Storm; in the 1980's it was Pop, Glam-Rock rap, funk New Wave, Punk, Techno, Dance Tracks, Heavy Metal, Hair Metal, New Jack Swing; In the 1990's House, Hip-Hop, G-Funk, Urban dominated. Now in the Millennium it is called Swag. Over the last few decades, most popular dance music, whether it's Pop, Rock, or R&B, the music has deep funk grooves. *P-Funk* greatly popularized this trend.

Some 70's artists remained true to this niche', others just passed through and onward with the new flavor of the moment, *Disco*.

When *Parliament* joined *Casablanca Records*, it was the only band that already had hit record success on the national music charts. What they needed was an owner to help let them expand their group brand and finance it. When *Casablanca* started as an independent label, they had that promotions and marketing visionary in Neil Bogart. According to George, at *Casablanca*, there was no competition, in fact they created their own unique niche so they would not have to compete with the other acts. However, there was some competition in the music scene on the music charts in the mid-seventies and that was Disco Music.

Disco Music, a growing genre sounded like a watered-down brand of Pop, R&B with a bit of Salsa beat and a bit of Funk in the dance music. It could also sound like a Las Vegas revue. The bands usually had 15 or more members, crazy costumes and sometimes songs about the most outlandish stuff. OK, some of the music lyrics were funny and on point like R&B artists *Joe Tex's, Ain't Gonna Bump No More with No Big Fat Woman* or *Jimmy Castor's, Bertha Butt* or *Wild Cherry's, Play That Funky Music White Boy.* Because Disco was nothing but commercialized R&B music, it dominated the airwaves, fashions, TV shows, movies and lifestyle.

In the 70's there were bands and solo artists like: *K.C. and the Sunshine Band, The O'Jays, Van McCoy, Dennis Coffey, Brass Construction, Brick, B.T. Express, Tower of Power, Earth, Wind and Fire, The Dazz Band, Lakeside, Commodores, Lakeside, Kool and the Gang, The Average White Band, Con Funk-Shun* and *Chaka Khan.* These artists dominated the R&B and Pop airwaves. Newer Innovators in dance music *like Bernard Edwards, Nile Rodgers and Tony Thompson* of *Chic* would have an influence in not only the popularity of Disco, but in Rap and Pop music over the next three decades. George loved the *Ohio Players*. He introduced them to Armen Boladian and got them signed to Westbound in the early seventies. Originally, they were called the *Ohio Untouchables* and in the early 1960's they backed a young *Wilson Pickett* of the Detroit vocal group called the *Falcons*. In the mid 1970's they had major hits on Mercury Records like *Fire*, a Billboard #1 hit in 1975 and *Love Rollercoaster* a #1 hit in 1976.

Stevie Wonder is an artist that had major success as a child musical prodigy, singer and songwriter with Motown label. Even with this success, he was not allowed to produce his own music until he let his contract expire around his 20th birthday. When *Motown* agreed to let Stevie create and produce his own music career, that freedom allowed him to write and produce Grammy Award winning hits like: *Superstition, You Are the Sunshine of My Life* and dozens more Top 10 hits. Another band that originated when *The Parliaments* first started having national hits in the late 1960's was the *Bar-Kays*, a group of teens whose early music was funky. In fact, their original members were the backup band for the legendary *Otis Redding*. They also worked with writer/singer *Isaac Hayes*. All of these artists had funky elements and some of them went on to have success on the disco/dance charts in the 1970's and 80's. Of course, there were other solos, duos and groups that had their R&B hits. But The *P-Funk* charted new ground through the 70's.

Meanwhile the trend of disco became a genre embraced by all races, straight, gay, women and men in the mid to late 70's. It also promoted a show of glamour and success thanks in part to Disco music.

One example of this was the opening of the famous New York club, *Studio 54*. When Steve Rubell transformed the former *CBS Studio* into *Studio 54* it was the place to be for a brief time. The club attracted music icons, celebrities and the club in turn became a celebrity worldwide. Music groups of the day were even having their names associated with and photos taken in front of the club by the paparazzi and mentioned in the media as *Club 54* goers. Movies about the lifestyle of disco became popular like *Saturday Night Fever* and *Thank God It's Friday*. That is until Steve Rubell was quoted in the New York newspaper in December 1978 as saying that *Studio 54* had made $7 million dollars in its first year and "only the Mafia made more money." Soon after that admission, the club was raided and he and co-founder/creator Ian Scharger were arrested for tax evasion. It was reported that they skimmed 2.5 million off the profits.

18
UnDisco Niche

Funk, a genre all its own in the 70's had elements of a heavy bass line, strong drumming, and funky horn sections. To make the definition easier to understand, you could say it is a combination of Blues, Soul, R&B and Jazz with emotion. *James Brown* is noted as influencing musicians and the world in the last 60 years about Funk music. Everyone from the *Rolling Stones to George Clinton* have noted *James Brown's* impact on them. But *James Brown* gave credit to *Little Richard.* In fact, some of James's band members, *The Famous Flames,* came from *Little Richard's* band when he left Rock&Roll to become an evangelist in 1957. *Little Richard* was influenced by *Billy Wright,* a jump blues singer known as the "*Prince of Blues*". *Billy Wright* shared the stage with one of George's early childhood music memories, an artist named *Wynonie Harris.* Harris was considered a Rock&Roll influence on many artists like Elvis Presley. *Hank Ballad's Midnighters,* the *Orioles and The Moonglows* and others carried the Soul/ Funk niche' forward thru the 60's and 70's. An interesting point is that T*he Famous Flames* were a band long before *James Brown* was asked to join them.

James Brown and The Famous Flames popularized their funk and soul music mix from the Southern States to the *Apollo Theatre.* Brown first recorded hits like *"Try Me"* in 1958. It became a hit on the R&B Charts. Hits like *Night Train* in 1962, charted #5 R&B and # 35 Pop and *Papa's Got a Brand New Bag* in 1964. It not only hit #1 but *James Brown* won his first *Grammy Award*. His backup players and singers were prominently featured on singles and in live performances. His backing musicians also went on to do solo work and became break out artists like J*imi Hendrix, William*

"Bootsy" Collin, Phelps "Catfish" Collins, Maceo Parker, Billy Byrd, Fred Wesley, Bobby Bennett, "Baby Lloyd" Stallworth and Johnny Terry among others.

The now famous *Funk Brothers* of *Motown* were a funky bunch. However, at the height of their fame, few people outside the music industry knew who they were. This group backed up every famous *Motown* artist and charted over 40 top 10 and top 20 charted hits in the 60's alone. It is George's opinion that if *Berry Gordy* had allowed the *Funk Brothers* to become household names, it could have extended *Motown*'s music influence and possibly extended their music hit streak as musicians as their featured solos and song were popular on commercial radio in the 60's and 70's. Bassist *James Jamerson* was a major feature on *Motown* hits. The *Funk Brothers* were used as background employed musicians. Even at the time span of *Motown*'s greatest hits they were not to be employed by other record companies. One of the company's writers, vocalist and *Motown Revue* MC's was *Shorty Long*, his name may not be familiar, but one of his songs is a classic! William Fredrick Earl Long wrote and recorded the first version of *Devil with the Blue Dress* in 1964. *Mitch Rider and the Detroit Wheels* took the slow blues song and sped it up to make it hit in 1966. Other funky hits by Shorty were *Function at the Junction* in 1966 and 1968's *Here Comes the Judge* a # 8 hit. Outside of *Smokey Robinson*, Shorty was the only artist allowed to produce his hits. At the height of his fame, he was killed in a boating accident in 1969.

The *P-Funk* organization was not really a part of the club scene or even TV scene in the 1970's or the 1980's, not even at the height of their fame. Their niche' was making music and over the top funk operas for their fans at their own live performances. And as the 70's moved on, Funk artists and concerts would prove to be profitable on their own because of the diverse audiences and clever marketing. Although there was talk of having *P-Funk* on movie soundtracks and even proposals for movies, a Funk-centered movie at that time was not to be. Top 40 radio was pumping disco music, but pockets of teens and musicians were paying attention to the genre of Funk music. This would prove to be a major asset in the coming decades as funk would dominate music for both black and white artists in the genre of pop, new wave, punk, rock, grunge, and the ever-growing popularity of Rap music internationally.

The Parliament/Funkadelic organization had Neil's approval and promotional support to create and grow their own tribe. Still the decadence of the music era was still a bit carefree, this included the *Casablanca* label's elaborate treatment of its clients and its workers. George says that there are differences in each music genre in terms of partying and drugs. With the Rock and roll business come the "Sex, Drugs and Rock and Roll" tag and groupies. Having done the LSD and the psychedelic stuff in the sixties and early seventies, the disco crowd tended to be upper class or wealthy and their drug of choice was cocaine. The crowd was also picky about the types or quality of the drugs. There was a tendency for this crowd to be into materialism. The flashy cars, clothes, jewelry, homes and over the top quality and quantity of those "things', or "toys" was important. The funk crowd tended to be poorer. Yeah, they wanted to look good, even sound good, but most likely they did not have the millions of dollars to spend on these things monthly, nor demand a certain "quality" of recreational drugs on a regular basis.

Most of George's drive in the music area was to make more music and get more resources to make more music, not get "things" or "toys". Drugs- yes, women-yes; cars, homes, jewelry, -NO! Also, the *P-Funk* organization was more like a family and not all just about individuals, at least in the beginnings of their fame.

In the Spring of 1977, a 45-date national concert tour with headliner's, *Parliament Funkadelic, Bootsy's Rubberband and Rose Royce* ended on April 10th. Those concerts netted over 2.4 million in sales.

In 1977, *The Mothership* and *The Clones* of *Funkenstein* had a commanding advertising budget welcoming their Funkateers to join them for the *P-Funk Earth Tour*. The group was tearing the roof off of America's largest concert halls. The music was recorded live for a two-album set that included a 22 by 33 full color poster of *Dr. Funkenstein* and an iron on T-shirt transfer with the motto *"Take Funk to Heaven in '77!* It was also the first album to feature vocalists Dawn Silva, and Lynn Mabry.

19
Casablanca Records Sky High Blow.............

Neil Bogart was attracted to originality. This is why he believed in artists like *Parliament, KISS, Donna Summer*, and others he signed and promoted. Casablanca Records and later Casablanca Records and Filmworks in the 1970's was known for its drugs, parties and over-the-top spending sprees. "There was blow everywhere. It was like some sort of condiment that had to be brushed away. Cocaine dusted everything. It was on fingertips, tabletops, upper lips, and the floor."

Bogart was a great promotions man and spent tons of money on record pressing and shipping. It seemed that on the books, Casablanca was always in the black. However, many of those records came back to him unsold! Sales were inflated and when PolyGram got wind that something was up, they investigated further to find out the truth. *Parliament* was in the "black" as far as music sales were concerned, way over acts like *KISS and Donna Summer* who had tons more promotion from *Casablanca*.

George says that *"Casablanca* was nothing but drugs." No matter where you went, cocaine was the request of the day. Everyone from business executives, Main Street USA, record moguls, as well as, DJ's. Besides coke? Weed, heroin, angel dust, Quaaludes and oh yeah, there was a whole lot of sex going on too.

In the book, *And Party Every Day: The Inside Story of Casablanca Records, Larry Harris*, mentions *Parliament-Funkadelic*. Larry is label co-founder and a cousin of founder Neil Bogart's. He says: "To look at Parliament and their absurd stage show- which eventually came to include an enormous UFO called *the Mothership* (which would land onstage in a billowing cloud of dry-ice fog) and a giant skull with a glowing four-foot doobie dangling from its mouth- you would think that there would be a never-ending series of strange Parliament tales to tell. To be truthful, the band was really fun to work with, and aside from a few battles of the kind that typically occur between artists and their record companies, everything went well."

Bret Alperowitz agrees with the notion of *Casablanca's* almost incredible opulence, intimidating that while many labels' executives in the industry during that era discouraged garish shows of money from their employees, *Neil Bogart* would get upset with his staff for not spending decadently enough. *Larry Harris* claims Casablanca "would have birthday celebrations with crates of Dom Perignon and lavish cakes for everyone, from the top-level employee to the lowliest mail-room worker."

By 1977, *Casablanca* had expanded its company to include films like *Midnight Express* in 1978,' *'The Deep* in 1977 and *Thank God It's Friday'* in 1978. The company's films would win two *Academy Awards* for music - *Mr. Giorgio Moroder* for his *"Midnight Express"* score, the other award to *Paul Jabara* for the movie theme for, '*Thank God It's Friday,*', called *'Last Dance.'* But even with their artists reaching chart-topping success and movies that were amazingly successful, the company was losing money, due to reckless spending. Still the party continued.

On the verge of success at the end of 1977, George explained his reasons for maintaining both groups and his future goal: "We were hungry and had to record and perform," says Clinton. He decided to split musically, two for one, developing a more vocal, danceable, and his biggest-selling group, *Parliament* (minus the s), for Casablanca Records and a gritty heavy guitar rock group, which kept the name Funkadelic, for Warner Bros. Records. "Now we'll always be two groups. If you're not getting along with one record company, you're getting along with the other—it keeps you from being ignored." His ultimate goal, George proclaims, is to be "the Black Beatles."

Multifarious Funk

20
P-Funkology 101

Clinton said "We had put black people in situations nobody ever thought they would be in, like the White House. I figured another place you wouldn't think black people would be was in outer space. I was a big fan of Star Trek, so we did a thing with a pimp sitting in a spaceship shaped like a Cadillac, and we did all these James Brown-type grooves, but with street talk and ghetto slang."

The use of a storyline to introduce new music characters was the focus of the next series of popular Parliament albums filled with Super-Heroes, aliens and spirit beings, all in character that brought the fans into a new galaxy. The story starts in 1975's album *Mothership Connection*. A divine cosmic being called *"Starchild"* comes to earth from his spaceship *the Mothership* to bring righteous *funk*-life & energy to all humanity.

Dr. Funkenstein was the leader character. *George says of* Neil Bogart, owner of *Casablanca Records,* "I had wanted to be with him for years because he was a good promotion man. But he would only do it if I would be the center of attraction. And I was reluctant to do that because that wasn't our style. I had heard that once before by *Dave Kapralik*, manager *of Sly and the Family Stone*. He thought it was too dark and you couldn't distinguish the focal point of the band, and that I would trust me more than anyone else doing that. So, I reluctantly said yes and that became *Dr. Funkenstein.*"

George wanted his spaceship, so his manager *Cholly Bassoline* got one from a prop ship in L.A. It had a unique history, it was the original spaceship from the sci-fi movie *"The Day the Earth Stood*

Still, a 1951 science fiction film from 20th Century Fox. It is on *the Mothership* album cover.

George recalls "When I told him [*Dave Kapralik*] after we got the hit record, you don't get paid for records in the tail end anyway, but you can get help with promotion. I said, "Buy me this spaceship," and I didn't have to finish the sentence. He went and got me a loan from the bank for a million dollars. Jules Fisher built the spaceship, did all the costuming. I told him we wanted to be able to land it on the stage…It was a funk opera".

Can you imagine a radio station that would NOT play Funk? Well, when you get fed up, you just have to create your own station. George did that! W-E-F-U-N-K is the station that has be loved for decades. Scores of fans started to follow the storyline of the albums, songs, even, *P-Funk Tours.* The marketing that George created along with *Overton Loyd's* renderings started a tribe of devoted followers.

"We landed the spaceship at five o'clock in the morning right in Times Square, right in front of the Coca Cola sign. With no permit in '77. The only person who came out was the DJ, *Murray the K.* He was ripped, he was drunk. He said, *"Dr. Funkenstein*, welcome to planet Earth. I am *Murray the K,* the fifth *Beatle."* It transported us for 10 years all the way up to *"Atomic Dog."*

On Sunday, October 23rd, 1977, *Parliament-Funkadelic* were on tour at the Convention Center in Pine Bluff, Arkansas with *the Mothership*. On the bill were the groups *Cameo* and *Brick*. In the late 1970's, the World-Famous Apollo Theater in Harlem was in disrepair and bankruptcy. *The Parliaments* had won many amateur nights there in their early career and many great entertainers graced the stage in the 1940's through the 1960's. In 1977, George and *Parliament-Funkadelic* brought an unforgettable show to the Apollo "He brought this huge spacecraft, a mothership, on stage. It was very strange, very out there," says Billy Mitchell. "And unforgettable."

21
The Dr. of Funk

The galactic story continues with the introduction of the divine *Dr. Funkenstein* in *Parliaments*1976 album *"The Clones of Dr. Funkenstein"*. *Starchild* was a protege' of *Dr. Funkenstein*, he worked with him in secret to help humanity by fixing man's ill's.

In the mid -seventies a book called *Clones* caught George's attention. There were even TV shows about clones. He also **researched author H.G. Wells** *"The Island of Dr. Moreau* and more books about cloning. He even looked at the studies that the government was doing regarding it. The P-Funk Empire was growing, evolving, so it was a theme that caught George's attention. He says "Along with the commercial implications, there was a spiritual part of the equation. In one book, there was an anecdote about how a woman in a lab had created a hundred salamanders from a single cell. That seemed fantastic and futuristic. But it also tied back to something I have been thinking about since *Chariots of the Gods*, which is that death can be defeated by science. If you're in ancient Egypt and you're embalming someone, keeping them in a state forever, that seems like a hope that you'll see them living again one day. Cloning was cutting edge science that answered age-old questions about morality."

In 1977, the cosmic characters are included in songs and in an illustrated comic book that was included in Parliament's *Funkentelechy Vs. the Placebo Syndrome*, portraying the now famous funk battle between *Sir Nose DVoidoffunk* and *Starchild*. The comic book explains the lyrics about *Sir Nose DVoidoffunk*, who is determined not to dance. He is ultimately defeated by *Starchild*, who is equipped with his Bop Gun, and when *Starchild* shines a flashlight on him.

In *The Clones of Dr. Funkenstein, Starchild* - Emperor of Funk has bullies that try to prevent him from his spread of the FUNK. Let's follow the story to the next album, *Funkentelechy vs. the Placebo Syndrome*. It was released on Casablanca in 1977. The bully *Sir Nose (Devoid of Funk)* is a finely dressed, super-uncool, irritating fool, who is too cool to dance, have fun and most likely too good to enjoy all of life's pleasures. He is the embodiment of the Placebo Syndrome- uncoolness and stupidity. Sir Nose has a goal to place mankind into a *Zone of Zero Funkativity*. He is conceited enough to think that we want to be HIM!

Luckily Starchild uses the Bop Gun on him so Sir Nose can reach Funkentelechy- freedom to dance.

Now I lay me down to sleeping
I guess I will go count sheep
Oh, but I will never dance
Sir Nose Devoid of Funk

Most of all he needs the Funk
(Shine the spotlight on him)
Help him find the funk
(Oh funk me)

Dance Nose! You know you on my funky street?
Oh funk me
Get down, Nose! I like it!
Dance then.

(Lyrics to *Flash Light*)

By 1978, The P-Funk organization had become a strong hit and tour attracting ensemble. It is this year that they would achieve their most professional and commercial music status.

The single *Flash Light* by *Parliament* was released in January 1978. It held the #1 position on the R&B charts in BillBoard Magazine from March 4th to the 28th in 1978. The single is from the album *Funkentelechy vs. The Placebo Syndrome*. It also reached #16 on the Pop charts. It was written by George, *Bootsy Collins* and *Bernie Worrell*. The song's classic bass line is performed by *Bernie Worrell* on three connected Minimoog synthesizers. George originally had Bootsy in mind to do the lead vocals but he passed on this track and handled drums. The chorus on Flash Light sounds like a stadium of voices.

Lead vocals were handled by bandleader *George Clinton*, while Bootsy's older brother *Catfish Collins* played rhythm guitar. On the single, *Sir Nose* gets his own nod on this song, in it we get to hear his defiant stand against the *FUNK*. It is listed as one of the *500 Greatest Songs of All Time*. The song has been featured in commercials, TV shows and sampled by various artists. *Flash Light* was ironically replaced on the charts by the hit single *Bootzilla* by P-Funkster *William "Bootsy" Collins*.

The *Flash Light* is used on *Sir Nose* to get him to dance.

When the band went on tour in 1978, the *P-Funk* troupe experience of having multiple hits in a short span meant more successful tour crowds. George said that he looked out into an audience crowd to see the place illuminated. Fans had flashlights and sabers that lit up the place. In Washington, D.C, when the band toured, there was a flashlight shortage in many locations in the city. Flashlights ………it was an item that George had not thought of. The bands marketing up until that point consisted of futuristic costumes, stage props, *P-Funk* mythology, albums, coloring comic books, posters, stickers, and the *Mothership*. But although the shows were a great publicity plan, the tours were not super profitable for the band. Now his fans were showing him a way to profit, that came from his own music hits!

Billy Sparks, years before he became an actor in Prince's movie *Purple Rain,* was a *P-Funk* merchandiser. In fact, George observed that some of the bootlegged merchandise he sold looked better than the official stuff. But George did not completely shut him down. He had his manager Archie Ivy cut a deal with the bootlegger and make Billy Sparks an official bootlegger. With the success of the tours, the P-Funkateers grew and so did their support for all things *P-Funk*

22
Funkology Movement

The next stage for the Funk troupe would also re-acquaint George with a new group member who would take them to another successful notch. *Walter "Junie" Morrison*, a keyboardist, multi-instrumentalist, vocals, songwriter, arranger, producer, joined P-Funk in early 1978 as musical director after having success in the early 70's with the *Ohio Players* and as a solo artist. Though primarily a keyboardist, Junie composed or co-wrote several of the band's hits in the later 70's. Morrison stopped touring with the band after 1981, but contributed to many subsequent albums. During his time with *Parliament-Funkadelic* some of his work was credited under the name J.S. Theracon.

In 1978 *Funkadelic's* next single was, *"One Nation Under a Groove"*, it was also the title track from their album. A great dance track, it peaked at #28 on the Billboard Hot 100, #1 on the Soul Charts for six weeks September 30, 1978 thru November 4, 1978. It was *Funkadelic's* first single to sell over one million copies. The anthem was named by *Jet Magazine* as "Song of the Year". In the US, the original album also included a bonus 7" EP. Overseas the album came with a 4-song EP, three songs on one side and a 12-inch extended of *One Nation Under a Groove*.

Multifarious Funk

PBS Independent Lens

Talk about a *Psyche-Funkadelic Thing*, the opening lyrics are familiar to fans of the *Temptations* song called *Psychedelic Shack*, released in 1968.

> "So high you can't get around it, so low you can't get under it"

This hit made the *Rock and Roll Hall of Fame's* list of 500 Songs That Shaped Rock and Roll. It is ranked No. 474 on the *Rolling Stone Magazine's* list of *"the 500 Greatest Songs of All Time"*.

The song was written by *George Clinton, Walter Morrison* and *Garry Shider*. Recording sessions took place at United Sound Studio in Detroit, Michigan. The song was recorded live on April 15, 1978 at the Monroe Civic Center in Monroe, Louisiana. *Walter "Junie" Morrison* was the featured keyboardist and songwriter of the album and *Michael Hampton* was the featured guitarist on *One Nation Under a Groove*.

Before *Gary "Diaperman" Shider* joined the group, he was a vocalist and former band member for gospel artists: *Shirley Caesar, The Mighty Clouds of Joy,* and *The Five Blind Boys*, among many others.

He is the lead singer on this track. It was used in the song *Stomp* in 1996 and won a *Dove Award* for *Song of the Year* for the gospel group *God's Property* featuring *Kirk Franklin, Salt-N- Pepa* and *Cheryl James.*

Multifarious Funk

23
Mega Tribe Support

A Funkathon of music groups hit mega popularity in the fall of 1978, especially at *Soldier's Field* in Chicago. Many fans from all over America camped out the night before to be the first to attend a concert billed "One Nation Under a Groove", Chicago's first ever Funk Festival. In attendance were 67,000 fans packed and partying for six hours at the stadium. On the bill were the groups: *Parlet, Taste of Honey, Con Funk Shun, The Bar-Kays and Parliament-Funkadelic! Bootsy* did not appear at this concert, although he was scheduled to. He was exhausted from touring and sat this one out. When vocalist *"Diaperman" Garry Shider* wooed the crowd by strutting the stage in his platformed boots and P-Funk landed their *Mothership with George Clinton* and rocked the # 1 anthems *One Nation Under a Groove* and Flash *Light*, the crowd went crazy with cigarette lighters. Funk needed no Disco, TV appearances or MTV, it now had its own Nation with its own Army.

G-Funk fans will recognize the hit from Rapper *Ice Cube*'s track Bop Gun (One Nation) from his 1993 album *Lethal Injection. George says* "Cube was probably the easiest of all, because I worked with him so many times. He did videos and records of mine, and I did the same for him."

When asked about Bootsy's contribution of playing drums on the hits *One Nation Under a Groove* and *Knee Deep*, George replied "If I was successful at that time, I was fucked up! I am not pretending to know what went down."

Multifarious Funk

24
It's B Bootsy Baby Baba

As *William "Bootsy" Collins* grew as an artist, he created a few popular characters, and alter -egos for his albums. *Psychoticbumpschool* for Children with teacher *Casper "The Holy Ghost"* was introduced on *Bootsy Collins* 1976 single *"Stretchin' Out"*. He became the ladies' man/ *"Rhinestone Rockstar Doll Baby Baba"* Called *"Bootzilla"* and on the 1978 album *Bootsy? Player of the Year.*

Multifarious Funk

> "I come equipped with stereophonic funk
> Producin' disco
> Inductin' twin magnetic rock receptors
> I'm perfect for bumpin', you see
> Just wind me up!
> Put me on your credit charge and at no extra expense
> Come with a remote control unit
> Oh yeah I'm programmable!
> On heck of a doll baby baba
> Bootzilla here
> Made by the makers of funky things to play with
> Trademark Funk-A-Tech incorporated Baba.
> Written by *George Clinton* and *Bootsy Collins*

About a month after the album *Funkentelechy Vs, The Placebo Syndrome* dropped in 1978, *Bootsy Collins* hit single "*Bootzilla*" was released. The song is from his album *"Bootsy? Player of the Year* which went to #1 on the R&B album charts. The single held the #1 spot on the BillBoard R&B chart for a week. The single did not hit the Hot 100 though. Ironically, it followed *Parliaments* hit single *"Flash Light"* which had been #1 on the R&B charts for 4 weeks. A little friendly competition in the P-Funk kingdom only heightened the popularity of both bands.

The world's first wind-up *"Rhinestone Rock Star Doll, Babby Baba"* and *"The Player"*, Bootsy's alter-egos expanded the *P-Funk* mythology, and made more dedicated fans internationally. *George Clinton* and *Bootsy Collins* are the producers of the album and it was arranged by *"The Player"*. The album contained a punch-out pair of star-shaped glasses, Bootsy's trademark.

Bootsy was in a legal bind professionally in the late 70's because the name *Rubber Band* belonged to a folk music group in California. So, the name was subject to a court case which it would cost his label Warner Bros. half-a-million dollars. George says, "The ruling stipulated that the label couldn't take the payments out of Bootsy's royalties, but they did it anyway."

24 It's B Bootsy Baby Baba

After the loss of the band name, he regrouped with his original crew and renamed them the *Sweat Band* on the 1980 debut album. It was produced by Bootsy and George, and was the first official album released on *the Uncle Jam label* in June of 1979. Another album by Bootsy was the solo album *Ulta Wave* for Warner Bros.

Next for *Bootsy's Rubberband,* was an album called *"This Boot is Made for Funk-N* on *Uncle Jam Records,* released on Warner Bros in June 1979. After the album release, Bootsy legally could not use the *Rubberband* name for a while. He did use the *Rubberband* name on the 1982 12" single release *"Body Slam"*. *Overton Loyd* did the artwork on the album and included an 8-page comic book entitled *"The Almost Finished Comic"* also drawn by Loyd. *Dr. Funkenstein and Starr-Mon* (George and Bootsy) produced the album. It is the summer of 1978 and *P-Funk*'s amazing stage show is featured in a national magazine. This publicity helps to grow their popularity.

"When the P-Funk conglomeration goes on tour, its show is a $275,000 production, generally regarded as the most spectacular, and one of the first super productions ever executed by a Black group. In addition to the space ship, there is a flame spitting UFO, a striped gold pyramid, a 40-foot apple hat, and a 20-foot pair of sunglasses. An entourage of semi, buses and vans are required to haul the equipment and the 80 musicians who comprise Clinton's "traveling university of funk." And high-strung fans in cities across the U.S. swoon at chances to join in Clinton's raunchy chant/lyrics that startled the record industry "Shit, goddam/ Get off your ass and jam."

On the heels of two number #1 hits, *Parliament* dropped another chapter on devoted funkateers. It's Christmas/New Year winter funk affair. It included the remedy to dance as moved along into another exciting level with the late 1978 release of *"Motor Booty Affair"*. Of course, *Sir Nose* is too cool to do anything but be a pain; he even hates to swim and hates WATER!! He and the *Bumpnoxious Rumpofsteelskin* attempt to sink any attempts for all in the galaxy to have a great time in this new album chapter.

Enter *"Mr. Wiggles"* He and his peeps of Atlantis can do the Aqua Boogies underwater and not get wet, and so does Sir Nose. In fact, the citizens dance so well that they raise Atlantis from the bottom of the sea to the top.

Dr. Funkenstein gives this degree to *Starchild:*

> "Gather the baddest *Master of Funksters* from throughout the Galaxy. We shall dance down Bimini Road to the Emerald City and do the Underwater Boogie until we get off at the funktion.............
>
> Hark and Mark forward: Be ye aware of the Motor Booty....... go wiggle." (liner notes)

The Motor Booty Affair album has an 8-page cartoon book and album covers that has punch out characters.

Aqua Boogie is another #1 R&B hit from January 20, 1979 – February 10, 1979. It stayed there for four weeks! The song is a single from the album *Motor Booty Affair.*

A record review stated, "Artist Overton Lloyd's poster of the character *"Sir Nose D'Voidoffunk"*, and an 8-page comic book that explains the concept behind the album and explained the characters in the songs of albums like *Motor Booty Affair* was in-genius. Overton was a long-standing friend of George's, and his work ranged from colorful sketches and paintings to fully-fleshed-out pieces.

The original LP was released in several different configurations. The debut release consisted of a gate-fold album cover, with Loyd's artwork on the front and back covers. His illustrations included cartoon portraits of some of the characters mentioned in the songs on the album, including *Mr. Wiggles* the *Worm* and others like *Queen Freakaleen* and *T.R.T* (The *Real Thing" McLean*). There was also a picture disk, with Loyd's illustration printed directly on the vinyl LP. Finally, there was a special edition that included cardboard cutout figures featuring Loyd's cartoon illustrations of most of the characters mentioned in the songs.

Loyd even designed costumes based on the theme and album's cartoon illustrations for Parliament when they went on tour to promote Motor Booty Affair.

In an ad for Parliaments *Motor Booty* album it says:

A Psychoalphadiscobetabioaquadoloop

> *Come To The Aqua—Boogie Funktion*
> *Your Hosts*
> *Mr. Wiggles*
> *Giggles*
> *& Squirm*

A list of at least 40 plus tour dates for the group is listed throughout the U.S. for January thru April of 1979, with May dates to be announced.

Of course, the ad featuring *Sir Nose* continues to remind fans that:

> *Parliament*
> *Partying Every night*
> *on Casablanca Records and Filmworks*

On *Parliament's Gloryhallastoopid the character of* Sir Nose wins one battle by turning *Starchild* into a mule and loses his powers. Sir Nose taunts *Starchild* with lyrics to various songs in the saga.

> "*humdrum, twiddly-dee-dum Starchild!*"
> "*Where's your flashlight?* "
> *Where's your Bop Gun?*
> *Where's the Doctor Starchild?*"

But the FUNK wins the battle because it is the "living source". *So we the clones were designed.*

Multifarious Funk

"*Big Bang Theory*", which reveals that the Funk caused the creation of the universe, though the only legible clue is the ethereal backing vocal line,

"*So we the clones were designed.* Sir Nose traces his ancestry on the 1980 album *Trombipulation.* His ancestors the Cro-Nasal Sapiens where a funky bunch. Upon learning his family roots, he embraces his heritage and passes it along to his son *Sir Nose, Jr.* On the hit album "*Computer Games*" released in 1982, Sir Nose is featured on the song *Man's Best Friend/ Loopzilla*. He exclaims:

"This sounds familiar! Let me stick my nose in it and see what I smell this time! Ahahahaha."

The character of *Sir Nose* is inspired by a real person George knew from a rival group he and the Parliaments did 'battle of the bands' with. *Sammy Campbell and The Del Larks* were from Plainfield. A

tenor by the name of *Berkeley Othello Noel* was a member of that group. George explains that the man was good looking, but his speaking voice was distinguished with a Peter Lorre sound. His personality was irradiating and manners dangerous. Razor and hatchet crazy. George discussed some of his crazy behavior, "Another time his car stopped in front of the barbershop one day, and just cut off. He jumped up on the hood and in that same high, wobbly voice, said, "I haaaate you" to the car before stabbing it."

Originally the character of *Sir Nose* was to be a darker character than what we know today. It was the input of Neil Bogart who suggested that he be more commercial, even caricature-like "But he kept his personal touch in there- if you look on his shoes, you will see a little sign that says "*Ouch*." That's a perfect example of Sir Nose being cool at the expense of comfort."

Any of life's pleasures were too much for *Sir Nose* who thought he was above it all! No dancing, swimming, women, partying, God knows what else! His attitude of grandeur says it all. But he is really just frontin'. The Flashlight and the Bop Gun set him straight.

Starchild and Dr. Funkenstein, The Children of Productions, Uncle Jam and other alter egos of *George Clinton's* creation and Overton's illustrations were genius. About a half a decade before MTV, the albums and comic book take the fans into the music and story. Most people know a *Sir Nose,* so this character became a hit with fans. The real inspiration for one of the groups well-known characters served time in jail, and appeared in the 1978 Movie "*Scared Straight*". Sadly, he has since passed on.

The 1978 anti-tour was George's way of stripping down the music, so the fans could hear *P-Funk* and some of the new spin-off groups like *Brides of Funkenstein*. They toured small 4,000 seat theaters and lost money, about $15,000 a week. The band performed in fatigues with no *Mothership or* costumes. Jet magazine asked WHY? George says, "It's worth it." "In order to stay fresh and off of an ego trip…."

25
The Funkadelica Thang

The next album introduces listeners to the nation of *Funkadelica*. In *Uncle Jam Wants You*, the Funk rules and can't be either stopped or labeled. The followers are led by the one and only *Uncle Jam*. Their mission is to rescue dance music from the doldrums (unFunkiness). The single *Knee Deep* was a #1 hit from October 13, 1979 –October 27, 1979. George is joined on lead vocal with *Philippe' Wynne* former lead singer of The Spinners, *Garry Shider, Walter "Boogie" Morrison and Jessica Cleaves.* Jessica was former lead singer of *The Friends of Distinction*.

The hit is one of the more recognizable *Funkadelic* songs and featured on many rap tracks from *De la Soul, Tone Loc*, TV Shows *like Different Strokes* in 1979, *New York Undercover* in 1995. In 1996 George joined Tupac on *Can't C Me*. In 2015, it was featured in the hit movie *Straight Outta Compton*.

The difference in the earlier *Funkadelic* albums are rather more ethereal and spiritual on the song *Mommy what is a Funkadelic?* a single from their very first album, that spirit set the tone on describing who a *Funkadelic* was.

> By the way my name is Funk
> I am not of your world Hold still baby, I will do you no harm
> I think I'll be good to you
> Fly on
> **I am funkadelic dedicated to the feeling of good.**

Funkadelica is a nation of nonstop funk on the 1979 album *Uncle Jam Wants You*, the galaxy of dancing *Funkateers* and pure FUNK rules, Uncle George is their leader! The song *Groovallegiance* is the pledge of the *United Funk of Funkadelic*.

> *Let me take you by the hand*
> *And spread the funk across the land*
> *It's not hard to understand*
> *Headin' for the master plan*

26
Expanding the Funk Empire

The success of *Parliament* allowed George Clinton to produce multiple groups. George had the artists and the players that were making great music and these groups had record deals with multiple record labels. George with *Funkadelic* and *Bootsy Collins* had their music on Warner Bros; *Parlet* was on *Casablanca Records*; *Bernie Worrel* had a deal will *Arista Records*; *Brides of Funkenstein* and the *Horney Horns* were on *Atlantic Records*. These groups were already on tour when in a December 1978 interview George says, "We brought you *Dr. Funkenstein* — get ready for **The Codfather.**"

The chair of the record label, Neil Bogart wanted a more refined version of George's other female group, *The Brides of Funkenstein*. *Parlet* became that group! George created the group from *P-Funk* veteran background vocalists, *Mallia Franklin, Jeanette Washington, and Debbie Wright*. Washington and Wright were the original female members in *Parliament-Funkadelic* beginning in 1975. Their debut album was entitled *Pleasure Principle* in 1978. Two other

Multifarious Funk

albums by the group were: *Invasion of the Booty Snatchers* in 1979 and *Play Me or Trade Me"* 1980. These albums were on *Casablanca*. The track *"Cookie Jar"* was originally written and recorded by original *Parliament* member Clarence "Fuzzy" Haskins.

Mallia Franklin was a vocalist with both *P-Funk and Parlet. She* was known as the *Queen of Funk*. Mallia introduced George to Catfish and *Bootsy Collins* in 1971. She is also credited with re-introducing *Junie Morrison* to P-Funk in 1978. She and George appeared in artist *Prince*'s last film *Graffiti Bridge* in 1990. Her first solo album was called *Funkentersepter, it* was released in Japan in 1995 on P-Vine. Some album tracks were produced by Eddie Hazel. She wrote, with *Snoop Dogg*, on the 2002 release *Suited and Booted*. Mallia was married to drummer *Nathaniel Neblett* of 70's group *New Birth*.

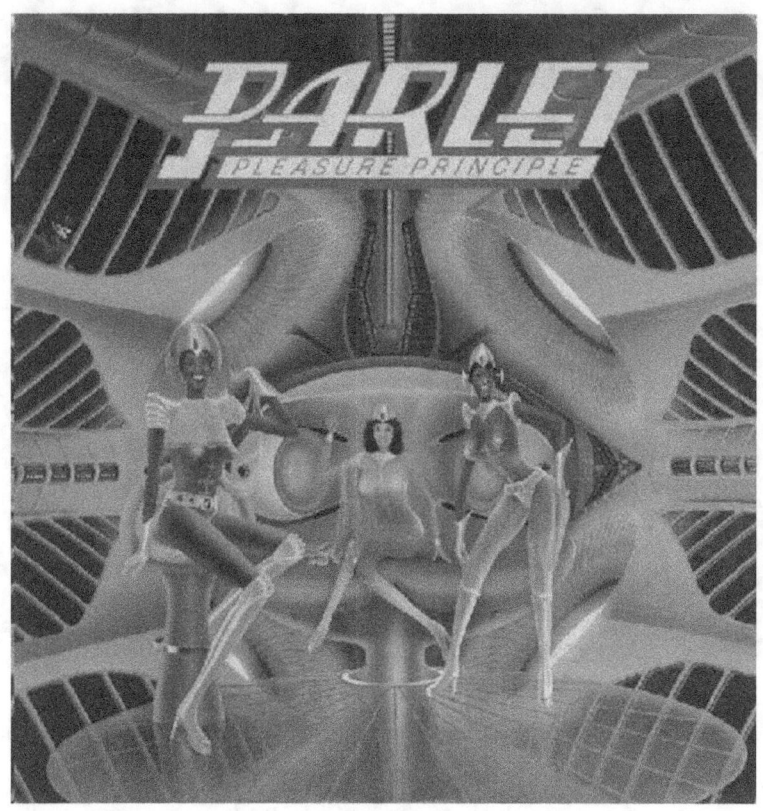

Multifarious Funk

The Brides of Funkenstein were a group that included former *Sly Stone* backup singers *Dawn Silva* and *Lynn Mabry*. George wanted a group that fit in with the theme of his *Parliament* album called *The Clones of Funkenstein*. Their debut album in 1978 was called *Funk or Walk, it was released* on Atlantic Records. A single from this album called *"Disco to Go"* was certified Gold in the U.S., but went platinum in Europe and Asia. They became the opening act for *Parliament* at the height of their popularity. They had two more albums *Never Buy Texas from a Cowboy*. It was rated by *Rolling Stone Magazine* as one of the 50 coolest albums ever released in 1979. A third album called *Shades on The Wall Shaped like the Hat You Wore* in 1980, was never released.

26 Expanding the Funk Empire

Multifarious Funk

Lynn Marby recorded with *The Talking Heads* in the 80's and *Dawn Silva* did back-up vocals for the *Gap Band* and *Ice Cube*. In 2000, she had a new album called *All My Funky Friends*. It was a hit in Europe and Asia. Today she continues to tour as *Dawn Silva and The Brides*.

26 *Expanding the Funk Empire*

Aside from their work with *Funkadelic*, *The Horny Horns* was a group that featured *Fred Wesley* on trombone, *Maceo Parker* on Saxophone, and Rick Gardner and Richard "Kush" Griffith on the album, Backwards in 1979. They contributed on albums by the *Red Hot Chilli Peppers*, *Freaky Styley* and *Deee Lite's* monster hit *Grove is in The Heart*. *Eddie Hazel* also had a solo debut album called *Games, Dames and Guitar Thangs* in 1977.

Philippe Wynne was a Detroit native raised in Cincinnati, Ohio. He started out as a gospel singer, then switched to R&B as a professional singer. He was in the *Pacemakers* with Bootsy and later did back-up as one of the *JB's*, *James Brown's* backup band. Philippe' would take over his cousin *G.C. Cameron's* spot in the group The Spinners in 1970. Although *Bobby Smith* was lead singer, Philippe's lead on hits like, *How Did I Let You Get Away* in 1972, was a #15 R&B and #77 Pop on the *Billboard Charts*; One *of a Kind Love Affair*, was a # 1 R&B and # 11 Pop in 1973; *Then Came You*, a song he shared lead vocals with *Bobby Smith* and *Dionne Warwick* in 1974, went #1 R&B and #1 Pop on the *Billboard Charts*; and *Rubberband Man"* #2 on the *Billboard Charts* in 1976. Philippe' was a featured vocalist on *Funkadelic's* #1 Billboard R&B hit *(Not Just) Knee Deep* in 1979. He joined Bootsy on his *Sweat Band a*lbum too. As a solo artist, his manager was *Alan Thicke*, Canadian Talk Show Host and actor, and music artist Robin Thicke's father.

27
Uncle Jam Records-distributed

The new deal George and his personal manager had with *CBS Records* for the label *Uncle Jam Records* included producing about 17 albums from the entire *P-Funk* collective. It seems like a crazy number of albums, but *Parliament-Funkadelic* groups had already charted success, producing as many albums and groups in 8 years. It was George's vision to have the biggest black-owned and run record deal in the world with all the talent run by his empire. In the November 8, 1979 issue of Jet Magazine, at an *Apollo Theatre* show, George said he was retiring and going to devote more time to producing albums and singles for his new record company, *Uncle Jam Records*.

Another development happened that concerned the touring troupe. Bootsy quit touring at the height of his fame in 1979. Although he had tens of thousands of screaming fans and was making about $ 100,000 a night from his tours. It was not fun anymore. Bootsy would return home from the road and in his private life not have the time to be just William Collins. In an article by writer Skip Tate in *Cincinnati Magazine* in 2000, he says "Once I started getting a clear picture of how the business works and how political it is, then I started not liking it because you didn't get into it for that," Collins says. "You just want to have fun doing what you do." He did not want the pressure which messes with an artist's creativity. Bootsy would not return to the road til about 1988.

Some artists on the roster had been a part of other chart-topping groups. For instance: Jessica Cleaves had been a lead singer with the *Friends of Distinction* on their 1968 hit called *Grazing in the*

Multifarious Funk

Grass. The group was discovered by football great *Jim Brown*. *Philippe Wynne* became well-known as lead singer on some of the *Spinners'* hits like *One of a Kind Love Affair* in 1976, *How Could I Let You Get Away* in 1972 and *Rubberband Man* in 1976. He shared lead vocal on *Funkadelic's (Not Just) Knee Deep*. *Eddie Hazel,* a *Funkadelic* guitarist was recording solo albums. Other groups included: *Brides of Funkenstein, Parlet, The Horny Horns and The Sweat Band,* Bootsy's re-named band. New group, *Zapp,* with lead singer *Roger Troutman*, from Hamilton, Ohio, joined up with *Funkadelic,* and built a promising relationship with George on a 1980 album.

On a TV show, filmed February 13, 1980 called *TV Party Live,* George was a guest along with pop star *Blondie* and *August Darnelle of Kid Creole and the Coconuts*. In this very rare TV interview, George talked about retiring. He also talked about appearing for a week stint supporting the community and fans of the *Apollo Theatre*. Later that year George would travel on the *Popsicle Tour* with the *Brides of Funkenstein*. George had the producers and musicians to make some outstanding albums. But his circuits were being overloaded with unprofitable tours, legal music deals that cost him tons of money. He would also experience artists wanting to use his expertise, take the credit, and backstab him in the process. Another chapter in this plot was just brewing.

Zapp

In 1979, *Zapp* was making their debut album for *Warner Bros. Records,* and Roger, a friend of Bootsy's, was working on songs for the group. The working title of one song was called "*Funky Bounce*". In its rough stages, George was not into it. With some focus on what would become lead singer Roger's trademark talk-box and organ, a section of the original was looped. Bootsy recalls, "*George Clinton* just happened to step into the studio that night and he really liked this one part that we had already re-did on *Funky Bounce*. He advised us to loop that section and put the other talk-box parts

27 Uncle Jam Records-distributed

over it. At that time, this was considered a genius act, because you had to actually cut the tape and make the right cut, line it up and loop it. So, let us not forget that the good *Dr. Funkenstein* was way ahead of this time, as well."

George gave Bootsy and Roger the producer's credit on the record. It was re-titled *More Bounce to the Ounce* in 1980. It reached number two on the Billboard R&B charts for two weeks in the fall of 1980. Roger was also to be a new artist with his debut solo album on the *Uncle Jam's* label produced by George. It was to be called *The Many Facets of Roger*. All seemed to be going well, but maybe Roger saw the problems that George was having legally with his label, bad financial skills and what many former band mates saw as poor managements practices and got his masters from Uncle Jam and took them to *Warner Bros Records*. The label offered Roger more money. However, George and crew had invested a lot of time, money along with CBS. In response to Troutman's uncaring move towards him, he says. "CBS paid for it, I paid for it, I don't like to go into it on the negative side, but it cost about 5 million [dollars], and a lot of people's jobs and what we consider as the empire falling."

Drugs! It was an issue for George and it hurt him professionally. With the shake-up at Casablanca.

In his book *Party Everyday,* author *Larry Harris* claims *George Clinton* and his "assistant" *Archie Ivy* would frequent the Casablanca offices, meeting with executives and rambling on "for hours about how they were going to develop *Parliament's* stage show into an otherworldly display of pageantry and pomp and how they needed half-a-zillion-dollars to do it." On some occasions, Clinton would show up with "some uncut and very potent coke, declaring that anyone who tried it would speak Spanish, as the stuff "hadn't cleared customs yet." The *P-Funk* front man, insists Harris, "would ramble on and on, giving voice to every thought that came into his head, stream-of-consciousness style, like *William Faulkner* gone jive."

But now in the late seventies, the Casablanca party was over and *Polygram* was losing money when they took over Casablanca. The company lost out financially and critically with their film, *Sargent Pepper's Lonely Hearts Club Band,* and its music soundtrack. This film included the *Bee Gees and Peter Frampton,* who were at the height of their popularity. It also included a Who's Who of music acts in the music industry like: *Earth, Wind and Fire, Billy Preston, Alice Cooper, Etta James* and *Aerosmith* along with other music greats. It is because of this failure and the death of disco coming within a year. A DJ who had been fired from his job at a rock station that turned into a disco station, decided to plan a *Disco Demolition Night* on July 12, 1979, in Chicago's Southside a*t* Comiskey Park. Participants were invited to bring disco 45 in vinyl records so they could be blown-up at the stadium. This event attracted over fifty-thousand devoted rock and pothead teens and young adults.

Although *Parliament-Funkadelic* was still on a career high with gold and platinum albums and hit singles, the dance music they were popular for was being shifted over to the disco genre although it clearly was not. And even though, George could still attract artists and create hits, his drug issues did not help him when the record companies were looking for reasons to cut artists and/or artists' support from their roster.

In the late seventies, while George was working with new band members and more with Bootst's band member *Robert "P-Nut Johnson*, he was also hanging out with his old friend and legendary funkster *Sly Stone*. He and Sly were working together on music and drug running together. One night he and Sly were busted outside a Denny's Restaurant while waiting for their coke to be delivered. But they had been sitting there too long. When he and Sly went to leave the parking lot, the cops showed up. The car was a cloud of smoke, evidentially the windows were rolled down. The cop's response was "If it isn't *Sly and Dr. Funkenstein.*" They went through the car, found nothing, but managed to get an old fragment of pipe from Sly's trunk. It was enough to hold us overnight. The

27 Uncle Jam Records-distributed

next morning, a friend of Sly's came down and got them out. Jail wasn't pleasant. It never was. But what was worse was the sense of being on the slide, with gravity increasing."

He felt the mounting responsibility of putting out new material and producing other acts. Although he shared the stage with other artists within the *P-Funk* dynasty, they did not step up and help lead. George was a great orchestrator. He had enough knowledge to put together compositions, players, showmanship, marketing, and attract new people, along with ideas to build a dynasty. He just did not have the people that wanted to do that with him nor maintain it. Another issue that happened with the members is one of separation. They did not work or collaborate together. One key thing to a successful venture is that even though there will be different personalities in the mix; you have to agree to disagree, but get along anyway. He says "On the other hand, as it turned out, people had trouble trusting each other. That was something I didn't understand. If you are going to learn anything, it's that you have to work with other people. You can't always ensure that your creativity is in working order, and people can differ on their opinions on a song. But damn, the basic shit that's required is that you get along, and work together."

Casablanca spent huge amounts of money on the *Mothership Connection/P-Funk Earth Tour* in 1976-77 and the *Motor Booty Affair Underwater Tour* in 1979. The label was doing great throughout the 70's with successful acts and successful films. In 1977, *PolyGram* located in Europe, acquired about 50% of the stake in Casablanca. Three years later, they bought the remaining stakes when they realized the lavish spending, was undercutting costs. Bogart accepted this transaction, but he was also removed from being CEO of Casablanca in 1980. In addition, in 1980 disco died, consumers stopped buying the records. Casablanca had branded itself as the Disco King, even though they had other acts that were not producing disco music. As a result, artists Neil brought in the company were left in limbo with no solid support in their music releases. For George and *P-Funk*, it meant no big budgets for promotions, shows or the CEO's support. The people running the label knew very little about how to work with music artists and that included the producers and managers they hired to work with *Casablanca's* established music artists who had unique niche's and who were million sellers. When Neil left so did *Donna Summer,* the label's biggest artist; *KISS* also eventually left. George and *P-Funk* were left without the solid backing or the marketing people who understood the funk genre or how to help build an audience.

The albums *Parliament* put out in 1979 *Gloryhallastoopid (Or Pin the Tale on the Funky)* and another album *Trombipulation in 1980* did not sell, as well as their previous albums. Because of absent promotions and budget support by the label, it missed the mark in having hits. However, both albums had above-average ratings from *Rolling Stone Magazine*. One single *Party People* is a song from the album *Gloryhallastoopid*. This single was released as both a two-part 7" single and a 12" record; it only reached #39 on the Billboard R&B chart. After years of warning *funkateers* to not compromise or fake the funk, they followed Uncle Jam's advice! The single sounded a bit too disco when you compare it to other *Parliament* jams. Music critic *Rickey Vincent* says that it is the band's "self-admitted worst record ever". George explains the meaning behind the *Trombipulation* album title. He read the book *Omnivorous Ape*. He wanted to expand the *P-Funk* Mythology in the story of *Sir Nose*. He had read that elephant trunks were their fingers. That piece of knowledge along with other elements would help him continue the character's story in the album.

Promotions for the albums came in the form of a cartoon promo for *Gloryhalastoopid* and talking chins for *Trombipulation! REALLY*, talking human chins made to look like faces that announced the album and music tracks. By today's standards this sounds silly *BUT* these marketing strategies and the comic books worked for fans and became interesting to a whole new growing audience. Future artists in the Rap world like I*ce Cube, De La Soul and Shock G* were all influenced by what they saw in the graphic and cartoons and heard as young kids taking notice of their parents and relative's album collections of music and album art.

The *Original P who* broke away from the P-Funk group a few years back, used the *Funkadelic* name to release their own album. The group included the original *Parliaments*: Fuzzy Haskins, Calvin Simon, Ray Davis and Grady Thomas. Their album 1980 album called *Connections and Disconnections* was released in Germany. In addition, bass singer Ray Davis began touring with the group *Zapp,* until the early 90's. This incident and *Uncle Jam Records* losing the master tapes of *Roger*'s album and him selling his masters to *Warner Bros* were other points that made the *P-Funk* empire look very shaky. The strong innovative brand that had attracted the major record deals in the 1970's did not work due to lack of capital to promote the genre of funk. It was not understood by most big record label executives who did not know the FUNK market. *Bernie Worrell* named the various issues that weighed the *Parliament-Funkadelic* empires, "Discontent" down. "Tired of all the unfairness. Being owed money. Lack of respect within the group. The management. Learning that money was stolen."

George and the *P-Funk All Stars* still toured, he had added some new members to the group. They did a week stint, *The Egg Tour,* at the *Apollo Theatre*. It re-opened very briefly after its closing in 1977 due to disrepair and with its re-opening in the early 1980's, he wanted to show support for the theatre and the community. It was under new management. In 1981, *Percy Sutton* and an *Inner City Theatre* group of private investors bought the theatre. It took some state funds to renovate the small venue. Many great black entertainers got their major start at the *Apollo Theatre*, too many to name but they include: band leaders *Lionel Hampton, Count Basie, Duke Ellington;* comedian's *Mom's Mabley, Redd Fox;* Doo-wop groups like the *Orioles, the Coasters, The Drifters;* soul icons, *James Brown, Ray Charles;* acts like, *Sammy Davis, Jr, the Motown Revue, The Supremes, The Temptations, The Four Tops, Stevie Wonder, a young Jackson 5 a*nd many, many, many, others got their careers boosted at the Apollo. But as these stars and others became famous, many did not continue to support the small 1,500-seat *Apollo Theater*, a Harlem landmark on West 125th Street that dates back to 1913. It was a former burlesque house theatre that changed to a popular theatre for African Americans to go for entertainment in the 1930's and 40's.

Percy Sutton, a Freedom Rider, member of the Tuskegee Airmen, and Civil Rights attorney during the 1960's, also owned the *Queen's Inner City Unity Cable System*. Sutton told the *New York Times* journalists Alan Finder and Anthony Ramirez, "The civil rights movement that I went to jail in was the same civil rights movement that killed the Apollo," Sutton said "We thought all the people who had started there and gone on to success would come back. But they didn't." Many famous black theatres where blacks in entertainment got their professional exposure were undergoing the same abandonment. *The Uptown* in Philadelphia, *The Fox Theater* in Detroit, *The Regal* in Chicago *and the Howard Theatre* in Washington, D.C., were all the major go-to venues during segregation. Many of these theatres also went into disrepair in the 1970's and 80's, shuttered for decades. It is only in the last ten to twenty years that some of these great venues have been restored. An example is the *Howard Theatre in* Washington, D.C. George was one of the artists that appeared after the venue was declared a National Landmark when restored in 2012; however, he and the *Parliaments* had first appeared there in 1967. Even in 2016, George continues to support historical black theatres and he also appears at these venues as a music guest, joining other contemporary artists. *The Uptown*, in Philadelphia is still raising funds to renovate and re-open.

Motown and its major stars along with other entertainers would return to *the Apollo* in 1985 for a history making event that was broadcast on NBC-TV. Another innovative move that *Percy Sutton* made was to revive the *Amateur Night at the Apollo* that the venue was so famous for. During his tenure from 1987-2002 the syndicated TV hit, *It's Show Time at the Apollo"*, was born. This brought international exposure for the venue as it brought young stars of the day, and seasoned icons like, *The New Edition, El Debarge, Mariah Carey, Regina Bell, Boyz II Men, Eartha Kitt, LL Cool J, Run D.M.C., Lauryn Hill, New Kids on the Block, Kirk Franklin, David Peaston, Digital Underground, Guy, Stephanie Mills, Melba Moore, NWA, Chris Rock, David Sanborn, Beastie Boys, Natalie Cole, Mary Wilson, Vanessa L. Williams, Hootie and the Blowfish, Billy Paul, Run D.M.C., DJ Jazzy Jeff and the Fresh Prince, Christina Aguilera, Billy Paul. BeBe & CeCe Wynans, Jeffery Osborne, Hall & Oates, James Brown, Ne-Yo*, and many more major artists back to the Apollo.

Back in Chocolate City, Washingtonian's braced for another mega-show from *Parliament-Funkadelic*. The show really made news with the fans!! "At a *Capital Centre* gig on April 25, 1981, Clinton stepped out of the *Mothership*, tossed his gold-lamé cape over his shoulder and strutted across the stage. "*Naked.*" Needless to say, the crowd roared in disbelief and amazement! Although the show was not filmed live, there is most likely a tape of this performance out there *somewhere*........

The other glaring issue of this story is that all in his camp knew and he could not deny: George was a raging drug addict! By the time the last *Funkadelic* album was made in 1981 called *The Electric Spanking of War Babies*, many of the players from the hit making era were gone, they had left the *P-Funk*. *Sly Stone* joins George, writing several of the songs on this album. It was the last to include long time core musicians & vocalists *George Clinton, Ray Davis, Garry Shider and Eddie Hazel. Junie Morrison* plays all the instruments on the title track. A guitar solo is played by *Michael Hampton*. It would be the last collaboration featuring *Junie Morrison*, *Mallia Franklin*, and *Jessica Cleaves*. *War Babies* is also the only *Funkadelic* album the late *Roger Troutman* contributed on.

The meaning of the album is a reference to the Vietnam generation. The album cover created by Pedro Bell is an amazing but censored work, his personal favorite. He says, "I made a mess of money on that one. The year was 1981, and the recording industry was awash in censorship, second guessing, and Tipper Gore-fueled paranoia. "They paid me to censor the cover," he explains. In the early eighties, the recording industry was targeted with mandatory censorship on album covers, from women's groups.

George's Clinton's debut album on *Capitol Records* was *Computer Games*, it was released November 5, 1982. Many of his band personnel from the *Parliament-Funkadelic* period to 1981, appear on this album; *Junie Morrison, Bernie Worrell, Bootsy Collins, Maceo Parker, Malia Franklin, Daryl Clinton, Eddie Hazel, Garry Shider, L Robert "P-Nut" Johnson, Gary "Mudbone" Cooper, Sir Nose D'voidafunk, Jessica Cleaves, Sub Woofer, Ray Davis* and *Dawn Silva*.

At the time of this album, George was going through professional and financial chaos. However, *Computer Games* proved to be a popular album, a major commercial success. *Although Loopzilla was* the first promoted single on the album, the breakout single *Atomic Dog* was a #1 R&B hit *on Billboard Magazine* Charts. The track *Loopzilla* hit the Top 20. He toured England, did the popular music show *Top of the Pop's* with *Grandmaster Flash*. There was even a video to promote *Atomic Dog* that won several awards. *Slant Magazine* named it, #97 on its list of *"Best Albums of the 1980s."* This song is the most sampled song written by George. It was also made famous a decade later by rapper *Snoop Dog* on his 1993 single *Who Am I?* (What's My Name)

Even with this success as a solo artist, George was struggling to stay clean while promoting the album on tour. He did go six weeks without crack, but never committed to himself that he was going to quit completely. George even took a rock of coke around with him to see *IF* he could resist it. With that sort of tease, he could not. An addict carrying around the very thing he is addicted to? At the end of the tour, that *ROCK* was his celebration! The effects of drugs were hurting his health and making him ill, but it did not stop him indulging.

In early 1983 George Clinton stated that his album, the first in about three years would assure fans that *Funkadelic* was still making music, despite a tiff with his former label *Warner Bros*. He was confident in *Computer Games* and his new singles. He said, "When you don't have records out and have hits, the public has to have some explanation People thought we broke up for a variety of reasons, but we never did........."

The reviews of *Computer Games* and the promotional tour were favorable

HE'S GIVEN FUNK A NEW MEANING

George Clinton, who will appear at the Tower Theater tonight, is the undisputed master of funk music, the gritty, rhythmic pop style that is now experiencing a resurgence. His new album *"Computer Games"* (*Capitol Records*) offers proof of why Clinton is considered one of the most innovative musicians in popular music. The hit singles on *"Computer Games," "Loopzilla"* and the current *"Atomic Dog,"* are at the same time dense (full of clanging guitars, a rumbling rhythm section) and light...*Philadelphia Inquirer* - March 26, 1983

Computer Games is not on-the-one with premium *P-Funk*, but for a nation hungry for grooves, it's a tasty side dish while awaiting the return of the mothership.

By John Milward April 28, 1983
Rolling Stone

Even though the critics were only warm to the album, *Atomic Dog* has become a classic hit that has been sampled by dozens of hip-hop artists over the last 30 years. George says "We were intentionally trying to sound like a hip-hop record when we did *Atomic Dog*. We had already begun to hear a little bit of the sampling and how songs were loose and disjointed form connecting grooves together, overlapping samples with each other. We very early tried to catch on to that. The songs that sounded electronic, we knew how to synthesize sounds. If you listen to the old versions, the B-side of it was us trying to rap. It sounded more like the *Sugarhill Gang*, but we actually did that as part of the remix of that song."

Other albums like *Urban Dance Floor Guerillas* and records like *Hydraulic Pump* and *Pumpin It Up* included guest vocalists *Philippe Wynne* and *Bobby Womack*. But these tracks were not promoted by the label. It came out on *Uncle Jam Records*. Again, George felt that people in promotions were not feeling his music buyers, and picking more pop friendly singles, not funk tracks that his fans were looking for. With no *Neil Bogart* executive-type on new or small labels, George was dealing with the corporate music industry that was stuck in a cookie cutter pop music groove, rather embracing a true funk mode. He was also now directly in competition with new artists and established artists.

It was at this time that the *P-Funk* Empire continued to be grounded along with the *Mothership,* because of lack of income and debt, caused by the disco backlash and other factors. *Tiger Flower,* the company that handled tours for them was strapped for cash. They also had the original famous *Mothership,* a 20-foot-wide heavy 12,000-pound structure that needed storing along with some of the band's music equipment. Now, many in the band were hard to get in touch with, to even ask, "hey, where can we send your stuff?" *Darryll Brooks*, a partner in *Tiger Flower* stored it in his family member's garage for a while until being demanded to move it. After not being able to get in touch with any of *P-Funk*, Brooks ditched it in a Seat Pleasant, Maryland wooded area junk yard. Brooks says. "Some of them were living with their mamas." When George heard about this incident years later, he was saddened. The Washington, DC area had always been career success for *P-Funk*, now their beloved *Mothership* that had been one of their trademarks was sold for its parts. It's reported that even some of keyboardist *Bernie Worrell's* gear was sold to local go-go bands. Although George was not happy about the *Mothership* being discarded like junk, guitarist/vocalist Garry Shider disagrees, citing the massive expenses that racked up from touring with an extensive entourage, elaborate costumes and a gigantic metal spacecraft. "I was glad it was gone," he says, "With the *Mothership* came no money."

An interesting thing about black music is that white artists have always admired the R&B/Funk genre. They were listening to George's music even when *P-Funk* music was not promoted by a major record company. Thanks to college radio, clubs and underground independent media who attract listeners willing to explore music off the mainstream corporate play lists, George and crew stayed relevant and he would soon be scouted out by an internationally diverse group of fans and musicians, literally!

In the 1980's, the tide in the music industry brought a new wave of change. George was cultivating new fans of his former hits, new music, and he was highly sought after for his expertise as a producer. Five years earlier, he stated that he wanted to produce new acts. And even though *Polygram* and *Warner Bros* were not showing him promotional support, young artists were very interested in seeking him out to produce them and paying him to do it! One of those groups was the *Red Hot Chili Peppers,* a group from California. The band's original line-up included *Anthony Kiedis, Flea, Hillel Slovak* and *Jack Irons*. The band became friends with Clinton and even moved to Michigan to work with him on some tracks. Both George and the Peppers had drug issues that played out during their working relationship. George says, "I had to get them an apartment in Detroit, because I couldn't have them getting in trouble at my farm," he says. "It was a small town, and I was doing bad enough myself. I remember thinking, 'Don't OD on me, please!' My friends would bring them back from the hood and say, "I know they your boys, man, but I'm-a try to rob 'them myself next time!"

Their album called *Freaky Styley*, was recorded at *United Sound Studios* in Detroit. The album featured original band guitarist *Hillel Slovak,* and musicians *Maceo Parker* and *Fred Wesley.* Although this album was not a great success when it was released, it became a collector's item when the *Chili Peppers* became hot 1990's artists. "George Clinton influenced me so deeply that it's like a part of me, like my kidney or my liver," says Flea of the Red Hot Chili Peppers. *The Chili Peppers* were inducted into the *Rock and Roll Hall of Fame* in 2012. Hillel was included in the induction.

George also worked with DeWayne Jessie, an actor in movies like: *Car Wash in* 1976; *Sparkle* in 1976 *Which Way Is Up? in 1977*; *Thank God It's Friday in 1978* and *National Lampoon's Animal House*. *Animal House* propelled DeWayne into a singing career because of his popularity in that film playing singer *Otis Day* with his on screen band *The Knights*. In that film, the group sang 1950's hits like *Shama Lama Dong Dong* and *Shout*. In the seventies to early eighties, there was revival of the early Doo-wop sound with music soundtracks like, *Grease* and TV shows like, *Happy Days*. Music stars of the 1960's, *Frankie Valli, Ronnie Spector, Gary U.S. Bonds* had top 10 hits on the charts again, and tribute sound groups like the *Bus Boys* became popular. In addition, *Broadway and* Theatre shows like *Beehive and Hairspray* were also popular. In keeping with the Doo Wop music genre that made them so popular in *Animal House*, George worked with DeWayne on an *Otis Day and the Knights* album of oldies as well as a redo of some early *Parliament* songs for *MCA Records*.

His other albums in the 1980's for Capitol Records are *You Shouldn't-Nuf Bit Fish, Some of My Best Jokes Are Friends, and R&B Skeletons in the Closet* and a live album *Mothership Connection (Live from the Summit, Houston, Texas)* and charting three singles in the

R&B Top 30, *Nubian Nut, Last Dance,* and a top *#20* hit *Do Fries Go with That Shake?* All these albums hit *Billboard Magazine's* Top Twenty R&B.

George worked with other artists and expanded his music into movie soundtracks and cameo appearances in TV movies and social causes. In 1985, South Africa was still under race separation, there were segregated entertainment venues and shows for whites and blacks. He participated in the *Steven Van Zandt* led cause by *Artists United against Apartheid* with *Sun City,* a protest song against apartheid in South Africa with many noted musicians like *Miles Davis, Bruce Springsteen, Bob Dylan, Bono, Darlene Love, Gil-Scott Heron, Herbie Hancock Hall & Oates, Run D.M.C, Tony Williams, Eddie Kendricks, and David Ruffin* among others. He wrote the theme song for the Emmy Award winning *Tracey Ullman Show.* George also co-wrote the theme song for the movie *Howard the Duck* in 1986, A collaborator from George's solo work, *Thomas Dolby,* also wrote music for the film. His film appearances included; *The Night Before in 1989* with *Keanu Reeves.* Other movies George has done cameo's in are; *PCU, Good Burger, House Party* and CBS-TV hit *How I Met Your Mother,* among many other appearances.

28
What is Funkin' Soul?

George was asked this question, "What is Soul?", in a 2015 PBS interview, He explained the different music genres of the last 75 years. In the first *Funkadelic* album he even explains it. "Soul is an evolving element that is expressed differently by different generations. It can be the same message, just expressed in real time to express/reflect what is going on". The soul in rap exploded in the 80's, although it was bubbling under the surface at least 15 years before. Some say the emergence of rap was started by songwriter *Clarence Henry Reid* aka *Blowfly,* his album, *Blowfly's Party,* hit the *Billboard* R&B *Top 50* in 1980; *Rapper's Delight* by the *Sugar Hill Gang* hit the *Billboard Chart* at #36 Pop and #4 R&B in January 1980. Some even say rap started 60 years ago and that some form of it has been passed down for centuries, heard in field chants, in school yards and playgrounds. In the 20th century, radio DJ *Jock Henderson* may come to mind when you think of early rap. I say *Pigmeat Markham's* Top 20 hit *Here Come's the Judge* in 1968 was pretty fierce competition for that honor too.

Another emerging genre George did not see coming was the evolution of rap, especially hip-hop music sampling *his music*. In 1989, a group from Long Island, New York called *De La Soul* had their first #1 hit on both the *Billboard* R&B and Dance Charts using *Funkadelic's* 1979 hit *Knee Deep*. George was caught off guard; he did not know what to make of it. The group paid $100,000 to use the song. This was just a taste of what was to come regarding young artists re-imaging his music. And it was an early sign of how established icons like he and James Brown would be celebrated in the growing pop culture. Many of the classic artists had limited music chart reach, only heavily promoted on the R&B charts and corporate controlled radio and media outlets.

Yet other music artists with classic songs did not always hit the pop charts on the first go round. The Top 10 *Just a Friend* by rapper *Biz Markie* is an example of this. It was actually a hit single in 1968 called, *You Got What I Need* for vocalist *Freddie Scott* and written by Kenneth *Gamble and Leon Huff*. However, with new life given to their hits by new young artists, *James Brown* and George have stayed relevant to a new generation. George loved what *De La Soul* did with their treatment of his hit *Knee Deep*. In fact, he appreciated the innovation of the new young artists in the way they used his songs. If an artist is true to the *P-Funk* philosophy, he is happy with that!

The commercial acceptance of Rap was slow and most thought it was just a short-term phase. But in 1979 the debut cross-over hit by the *Sugar Hill Gang* called *Rappers Delight* made use of rap and joined it with the backdrop music of the group *Chic*'s #1 hit *Good Times*. It was danceable enough to make the Dance/Disco charts in 1979. This type of rap was the commercial transition into the mainstream. It made the Top #5 in 10 countries and #36 on the U.S. Billboard charts. This genre of early rap became popular thanks to independent labels. It extended the genre of funk in ways no one could have predicted and transformed the emergence of *Go-Go* music in the mid to late 80's.

It could also bring social messages like in the *Grandmaster Flash* hit *The Message;* Run D.M.C.'s *It's Like That* and Curtis Blow's hit *The Breaks*. George's hit *Atomic Dog* in 1982 blew open the possibilities of funk married with rap into a new genre. In the late 80's *New Jack Swing* rhymes and the social consciousness grooves of *Public Enemy, A Tribe Called Quest,* and other artists used samplings of George, *P-Funk* and James Brown, song loops to hook listeners and make top 10 hits. Many new Millennial fans will only know of the original recording through new young artists using them in their song re-imaginations. It is because of this that George gives rap credit for his longevity. In 1991, *Digital Underground* invited George to be a guest on their 1991 *Sons of the P* which was certified Gold by the R.I.A.A. He also appears on the title track.

Multifarious Funk

29
Purple Reign

"There were only a few stars who carried the torch for raw funk in the mid-eighties, and the baddest of them all was *Prince*"

—George Clinton

At the height of *P-Funk's* popularity in the late 70's, a fan by the name of *Prince Rodgers Nelson* was just getting his music demos into major record labels. One of those labels was *Warner Bros.* It was at this time that George introduced his music to a popular DJ named the *Electrifying Mojo* in Detroit and he introduced his Detroit and Canadian listener to *Prince.* Mojo would play *Prince's* albums without interruption. After *Prince* hit music success, and after a birthday gig in the mid 80's, *Electrifying Mojo* got a rare interview with him on his radio show in the mid-eighties. In the interview, he said he considered Detroit as a second home.

For a time, George signed with *Prince's Paisley Park Records.* It was financed in part by *Warner Bros. Records.* Its record label was formed in 1985 after the major commercial success of *Prince's* movie *Purple Rain.* The label shared its name with the song *Paisley Park* from his album *Around the World in a Day,* which hit #1 on *the Billboard Album chart* in the spring of 1985. *Prince* was a longtime fan of *Parliament - Funkadelic,* he even attending concerts as a teenager, years before signing a recording contract with *Warner Bros* in the late 70's. At Paisley, George recorded two albums and *Prince* respected George enough to let him create his music while at the label. George and *Prince* collaborated on the song, *We Can Funk,* for the movie *Graffiti Bridge* in 1990. George also made an appearance in the movie.

His first album was *Cinderella Theory*. *Prince* also does background vocals on the album. *Hey Man...Smell My Finger,* his second album for Paisley Park, George samples himself. One of the most interesting and well-known singles from the album was *Martial Law* in 1993. It was produced by Kerry Gordy son of *Berry Gordy* and his first wife *Raynoma*. It was Raynoma that gave George his songwriting opportunity at J*obette* in 1963. There was a promotional video for *Martial Law.* Some album guests included: *Anthony Kiedis and Flea of the Red Hot Chili Peppers, Chuck D, Flavor Flav, Shock G of Digital Underground, Ice Cube, N'Dea Davenport, Dr. Dre, Yo-Yo, MC Breed, and Herbie Hancock,* as well as former *P-Funk* players, *Bootsy Collins, Bernie Worrell, Maceo Parker, and Fred Wesley.* In addition, *Prince's* own band members *Eric Leeds and Atlanta Bliss,* as well as *The Steeles,* performed on the album.

George and the P-Funk All Stars played *President Bill Clinton's* first inaugural "Youth Ball" in 1993. They also were a featured band for the Olympic Festivities in Atlanta, Georgia. *Chelsea Clinton,* a fan met George back stage with the Secret Service. The two posed for an official picture, he had a crack pipe in his hand he was concealing when that picture was taken. It was in *People Magazine*.

George signed with *Sony 550* and released *T.A.P.O.A.F.O.M. (The Awesome Power of a Fully Operational Mothership)* in 1996, and has had several live concert albums over the years. In 1996, George Joined Rap Icon *2Pac* in the studio for the track *Can't C Me f*rom his Diamond certified album *All Eyez on Me* in 1996. George *says* "2Pac was cool. I knew him from Digital Underground, so it was always easy to work with him."

30
A Parliafunkadelicment Thang

In 1997, George and *Parliament-Funkadelic* were inducted in the *Rock and Roll Hall of Fame*. They were presented their honor at the live ceremony by Pop and Soul icon *Prince*. It was interesting to look at George and *The Parliaments'* careers in the 1950's and 1960's. Back then they wanted to mimic their teenage idols and later other hit makers of the day at *Motown Records*. It was only when they evolved and became themselves that they became stars in their own right. Over the last thirty-five years, they have grown an army of fans in a way that none of their influences have. It is ironic that another group inducted in that same ceremony was *Motown*'s the *Jackson 5*. They gave their thanks to Motown founder *Berry Gordy* who was also at this ceremony.

The *P-Funk* inductees were:

Rock and Roll Hall of Fame Inductees

PARLIAMENT-FUNKADELIC

Inductees: George Clinton (vocals; born July 22, 1941)

Jerome "Bigfoot" Brailey (drums; born August 20, 1950)

William "Bootsy" Collins (bass, vocals; born October 26, 1951)

Raymond Davis (vocals; born March 29, 1940; died July 5, 2005)

Tiki Fulwood (drums, vocals; May 23, 1944; died October 29, 1979)

Glenn Lamont Goins (vocals, guitar; January 2, 1954; died July 29, 1978)

Michael Hampton (guitar; born November 15, 1956)

Clarence "Fuzzy" Haskins (vocals; born June 8, 1941)

Eddie Hazel (guitar, vocals; April 10, 1950 - December 23, 1992)

Walter "Junie" Morrison (keyboards, synthesizers; born 1954; died January 21, 2017)

Cordell "Boogie" Mosson Jr. (bass; October 16, 1952; died April 18, 2013)

William "Billy Bass" Nelson Jr. (bass; born January 28, 1951)

Garry Shider (vocals, guitar; born July 24, 1953; died June 16, 2010)

Calvin "Thang" Simon (vocals; born May 22, 1942)

Grady Thomas (vocals; born January 5, 1941)

Bernie Worrell (keyboards, vocals; born April 19, 1944; died June 24, 2016)

31

Evolving Funk

George and *Parliament -Funkadelic's* influence on music artists and new music over the last few decades has been enormous. They are too many to list in this book; however, they are people of all cultures and nationalities. George has greatly impacted pop culture. In addition, the young music loving audience is more urbanized now than they were when *The Parliaments and the Funkadelic's* started their *Parliafunkadelicment Thang!* In the eighties, many *P-Funk* musicians worked with other new groups emerging on the scene. Some examples are: *Bernie Worrell* worked and toured with the *Talking Heads*. They had an enormous hit with *Burning Down the House*. Its song title came from a chant drummer, *Chris Frantz* heard at a *Parliament-Funkadelic* concert. *Garry "Mudbone" Cooper* formed a duo with singer *Michael Camacho* called *Sly Fox*. They had a #7 hit called *Let's Go All the Way* in 1985; the group *Deee-Lite* featured grooves by *Bootsy and Catfish Collins* and others on the 1992 top 10 hit *Groove is in the Heart*.

There are a few generations of rap, hip-hop and Funk artists that Clinton and P-Funk have influence. Some include: Uncle Jamm's Army, Prince, Dr. Dre, Prince Charles and the City Beat Band; Mike Watt, Red Hot Chili Peppers, Fishbone, Maurice Starr; Beastie Boys, De La Soul, Tone Loc, A Tribe Called Quest, TuPac, Digital Underground, Public Enemy, Prince Paul, Snoop Dogg, Biggie Small, OutKast, Missy Elliott, Meshell Ndegeocello, D'Angelo, Lil' Kim, Fred Durst, and Mix Master Mike Erik B. and Rakim, MC Hammer Digital Underground, Ice Cube, Warren G, Kirk Franklin, Kendrick Lamarr, Nipsey Hussel...............the list goes on into 2017, 2018, 2019, 2020 and beyond.

He ranks second on the list of most-sampled artists in music history, with more than 400 times to date, including as singer, writer and producer of *Parliament, Funkadelic, Bootsy Collins and Bootsy's Rubber Band*. His top five sampled songs include at number 5): *Flash Light, sampled* about 60 Times; Number 4) is *Mothership Connection-(Starchild)* 28 Times; Number 3) is *I'd Rather Be with You*, it has been sampled about 30 times; Number 2) is *Knee Deep*, sampled about 70 times; And at number 1) is *Atomic Dog*, sampled about 150 times!! So even after George had his last top-charting hits with his groups and as a solo artist, throughout the last thirty-five years, George has been on the music charts or some place of prominence in the media, forever!!

The rise of sampling in popular music gives life to classic hits and the artists who made them famous. George feels that this is a good thing, as opposed to having his hits delegated only to an oldies music compilation sold on TV. He is even a guest on singles and albums of present day artists. In 2017, George has new music on the charts; in 2016, he joined *Nipsey Hussel* and *Snoop Dogg -Da Young Fellaz* on the track *Do The Damn Thang*. As for his views on new artist versus old artists, he believes that there is no past or present, just transformation. He says, *"Funk is forever moving."* He is not afraid to explore new music styles, new artists, but is eager to learn from and embrace the evolution. This attitude has kept his career moving forward.

In addition to their Rock Hall Induction, *P-Funk* also received a 2002 Lifetime Achievement Award at the N.A.A.C.P. Image Awards. In 2005, the PBS series, *Independent Lens* profiled *Parliament Funkadelic, One Nation Under a Groove*. The filmmaker, *Yvonne Smith*, created animation based on *P-Funk* lyrics. A cartoon outer space being who serves as the film's narrator is called *Afronaut*. He comes to earth in the new millennium in the *Mothership* in an otherworldly intergalactic environment. *Afronaut* is voiced by comic actor *Eddie Griffin*. This profile lets fans and the curious see the faces and hear from various members of the group, managers and roadies about their experiences behind the scenes and in the music industry over the decades.

When George celebrated his 50 years in show business, in 2006, he recorded songs with his friends *The P-Funk All-Stars, Joi, Bobby Womack and Prince*. He has never stopped touring in the United States and internationally, and usually packs the venues with fans of every culture, gender and nationality. At that time, George was still creating and had no intention of stopping. He said" I ain't finished, so I can't be elated yet. To me, when you get to happiness, you ain't got nothing to do, but go somewhere and get fat and be bored. I know I'm fat, but I ain't bored yet" In 2012, George received an Honorary Doctorate Degree of Music from *Berklee College of Music*. In addition, he runs a successful fundraising campaign to digitize his *Parliament-Funkadelic* catalogue.

In 2014 George's Biography, *Brotha's Be like "Yo' George, Ain't that Funkin Kinda Hard on You,* came out. While writing his memoirs, he was thinking of his son George III, who had died in 2010. The *Emperor of Funk* was on the road again in Canada for a couple weeks, one date was at the *Phoenix Concert Theatre*. It had only been two weeks after his 50-year-old son, George Clinton III passed away. "He'd been sick for a while, his kidneys and liver. He was sick a long time, so we had a chance to prepare for it. I lost my mother a little over a month ago. I don't go to funerals."

He also reflected on others in the *P-Funk* family that have passed on. His history in the business of music is one that he wants his family and others to learn from. He had learned from his partying ways and cleaned up his lifestyle. Clinton's legs had swollen grotesquely, thanks to the baking soda used in crack. In 2011, he was rushed to a Los Angeles hospital after partying with Sly. He stayed for a week. The years of drug abuse had deteriorated his health, putting stress on his heart and lungs, among other health related issues. During his time alone, he had time to improve his health, transform his music career and personal future. Fred

Wesley said, "I don't know why he's still alive, or how his mind is still together,". "I used to smoke with him, and I quit years ago. I'm sure it would have killed me or an average person. George is amazing." The first thing Clinton does each morning is pick up the binoculars at the foot of his bed and gaze out the window at nature, the birds and squirrels.

He is a father, grandfather and great grandfather now and some of these young family generations also join George in the studio and on stage. His new music called *First You Gotta Shake the Gate* was included in his memoirs; the album artwork was illustrated by Pedro Bell. The music featured tracks by his children and grandchildren, with music by Holland Dozier Holland, a track with the late Jessica Cleaves and his close friends Sly Stone, Sidney Barnes; vocalists Belita Woods, the late Garry Shider, and his son Garrett Shider. Vocalist's, Kendra Foster, Steve Boyd, Robert 'P-Nut' Johnson, El DeBarge, Tracey Lewis, Kandy Apple Redd, Tonysha Nelson, Patavian Lewis, Kim Manning, Lashonda 'Sativa Diva' Clinton, Kim Burrell, Rob Manzoli and Del the Funky Homospian.

In *Pop Culture* the *P-Funk* Mythology is also becoming a part of historical culture. In 2012, it was announced that George Clinton's famous *Mothership* was going to be an exhibit at the *Smithsonian!* It was included in a section of the *Smithsonian's National Museum of African History and Culture.* An example of art and pop culture imitating *P-Funk* is in a 2015 episode of *Dr. Who,* a British science fiction show aired on the BBC, when a character referred to himself as *Dr. Funkenstein.*

32
United Sound Systems Recording Studios

The Parliament-Funkadelic sound was born and nurtured at *United Sound Systems Recording Studios*. It has become an institution which birthed a musical legacy and now it includes a museum. It is located on 5840 Second Avenue, Detroit, Michigan. Founded by *Jimmy Siracuse* in 1933, it became the first independent and full service major recording studio in the nation and created a platform which gave artists, musicians, writers, and producers the ability to record music, cut the record and get airplay without being signed to a major label. It was the place for advertisers to record for commercials and advert jingles, in the 1940s. Music greats like Charlie Parker, Max Roach & Miles Davis recorded BeBop Jazz Standards, and John Lee Hooker recorded 'Boogie Chillun'. Little Willie John, Jackie Wilson and songwriter Berry Gordy recorded Tamla/Motown's first release at this studio in 1959 called *Come to Me* by vocalist Marv Johnson.

Throughout the 1960s, the studio helped bring hits by artists like, *Bob Seger, (Ramblin' Gamblin Man)* in 1968; *The MC5, (Back In the USA)* in 1970; *Isaac Hayes* 1969 album *(Hot Buttered Soul)* and in 1971 *(Shaft); the Dramatics (Whatcha See Is Whatcha Get)* in 1971; *Johnnie Taylor's (Who's Makin' Love)* in 1968, the very first R.I.A.A. certified Platinum Single by *Johnnie Taylor (Disco Lady)* in 1976. In the 1970s artists *Gladys Knight and The Pips, Albert King, and Al Hudson and One Way* recorded music at United Sound.

Multifarious Funk

George recorded many albums and hits for *Parliament-Funkadelic*, they included: *Give Up The Funk (Tear The Roof Off The Sucker)*, *Mothership Connection, Flashlight, One Nation Under A Groove, (Not Just) Knee Deep* and *Atomic Dog*. In addition, spin-off *P-Funk* bands such as *Bootsy's Rubber Band, The Brides Of Funkenstein, Parlet, Fred Wesley & The Horny Horns* in the 1970's and 1980s. George was contacted by *The Red Hot Chili Peppers* and he produced their first major album in 1985 *Freaky Styley* at United Sound. Within the 1980s and 1990s, hits like *Luther Vandross, (A House Is Not a Home)* in 1981 and *R-Kelly's (I Believe I Can Fly)* in 1996, was recorded there with prominent *Motown* orchestra arranger Paul Riser. This studio is one of the few Detroit recording studios to still exist. George was a headliner at the studio's open house in 2013 and was very pleased that the studio is now a museum. He did a personal appearance for his memoirs there and also donated a restored 1920's Chickering Piano at the museum in 2014.

33
George Clinton

In the millennium, George is busier than ever. At the 58th annual *Grammy Awards* in 2016, singer *Bruno Mars* and songwriter/music producer *Mark Ronson* received the *Song of the Year Award* for *Uptown Funk*. From the stage, *Mark Ronson* introduced the audience to George who was seated in the room as a Funk pioneer. He collaborated with *Grammy Award* winning artist *Kendrick Lamar* on the single *Wesley's Theory* from the 2015 album *To Pimp a Butterfly*. The album was nominated for 11 Grammy Awards in 2015 and Kendrick won 5. The soundtrack for the hit movie *Straight Outta Compton* includes several *Parliament-Funkadelic* hits. Rapper's Ice Cube and Kendrick Lamarr joined George in the intergalactic themed video for his single *Ain't That Funkin' Kinda Hard on You?* Again, these in the now music collaborations mixed with George's classic music brings in a present-day generation who are hearing his music for the first time. Who knows, it may also spawn a new future Funk genre of music tracks.

As far as contemporary music, George is a forward thinker and opened to every music genre whether it is *grunge, rap, soul, pop, funk, rock*, whatever. He says: "Loved *grunge*. That serious, soulful sound? Cobain reminded me of *Eddie Hazel. Soundgarden?* Oh, my God. I loved that shit." He has worked with rock bands like *Lollapalooza, Phish,* and vocalist *Louie Vega* and *Soul Clap*. He remembers *Eminem* as a young kid just starting to find and perfect his craft. George says, "Eminem is one funky white motherfucker. I remember Eminem hanging around the studio when he was 14 years old. He was the baddest little dude and he still is today. He's unstoppable and true to the shit. He'll bust your head open with his rhymes."

He also put to rest the controversy regarding singer/songwriter *Robin Thicke's #1* hit *Blurred Lines.* Some music owners felt that a few bars of George's 1974 *Funkadelic* song *Sexy Ways* was copied along with *Marvin Gaye's* 1977 hit *Got to Give It Up*. George was quick to tweet that he disagreed with the controversy. He also believes that music labeled black or R&B some 40 years ago is now considered Pop today, and that includes Hip-Hop. The *Song of the Year* in 2015 is a good example of this. It is a tribute to groups like *The Time, Morris Day* and the *Gap Band,* that would have been played only on the R&B stations, receiving only limited play on the Pop Charts.

Uptown Funk You Up, Uptown Funk You Up
Lyrics from *Uptown Funk*
by *Mark Ronson* and *Bruno Mars* 2015

Oops Upside Your Head, Say Oops Upside Your Head
Lyrics from the 1979 single *I Don't Believe You Want to Get Up and Dance*
by *The Gap Band*

Although thirty-six years apart, **Yes**, that hit sounds very familiar! *The Gap Band also* received writer's credit for that 2015 *Grammy Award* Winning *Song of the Year!*

George was asked about the Internet and musicians getting their music out to the masses. He agreed that it was a great way for artists because he felt that record companies were not doing much for artists. Even if an artist sold a few, they could get paid. It is interesting that when something goes viral, it can become new to the viewer and listener. Many hours of film footage of *Parliament-Funkadelic* Tours and music from the 50's 60's and 70's are on the Internet. It is new to me and a lot of fun to watch and I am sure others have become familiar with the group too. George says: "Little, big, when you don't top the charts anymore, does that mean that everyone's over you? Or are there other ways to get over?" he goes on to say "Look at kids nine to nineteen. Pay attention to where they find their enthusiasm. These days it's on YouTube. They spend hours looking for the silliest thing, and that's what they decide to admire. That's what they decide to imitate. And it's that world where *P-Funk* is resurfacing now.

When *Kendrick Lamarr* and George first started working together, he really felt the spirit of what Kendrick was creating, he says "When you talk about your old work with a young man with an old mind, the work feels less old. We talked about my old songs and they were renewed. When the past comes rushing into the present that way, I can see clearly that artwork is a living thing."

George says he looks for stuff that gets on his nerves because it is the "next big thing". He also believes that artists with bands will make a comeback because you can only sample so much. With a band creating new sounds, the funk will always stay fresh. He is creating new music for *Parliament's* next album called *Medicine's Broad Dog*. Through his friendship and professional relationship with Lamarr, George was introduced to *Flying Lotus* who will also appear on the album.

George shows no sign of slowing down, He says "The funk itself, that's the energy. If I don't work I'm going to get tired," he says. "We're just getting started."

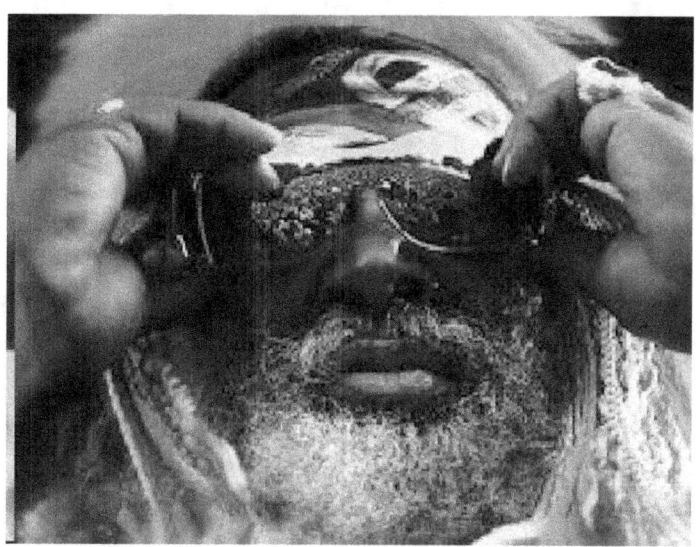

Multifarious Funk

References

Funk: The Music, The People, and The Rhythm of The One
By Rickey Vincent
Series: Funk: the MUSIC, the PEOPLE, and the Rhythm of THE ONE
Paperback: 416 pages
Publisher: St. Martin's Griffin (April 15, 1996)

Brothas Be, Yo Like George, Ain't That Funkin' Kinda Hard On You?: A Memoir Hardcover – October 21, 2014
by George Clinton (Author), Ben Greenman (Contributor)
Hardcover: 416 pages
Publisher: Atria Books (October 21, 2014)

George Clinton and P-Funk: An Oral History (For the Record)
Paperback – June 1, 1998 ;
Davis Mills (Author) Dave Marsh (Editor)

George Clinton & The Cosmic Odyssey Of The P-Funk Empire
Hardcover – August 1, 2014
by Kris Needs (Author)
Hardcover: 352 pages
Publisher: Omnibus Press (August 1, 2014)

"Extended Play: Sounding Off From John Gage to Dr, Funkenstein"
author John Corbert

Funk,
by David Thompson, Third ear: the essential listening companion
Backbeat Books, San Francisco, 2001
Thompson, Dave (2001). Funk. Backbeat Books.
ISBN 0-87930-629-7. p. 90.

Kempton, Arthur (2005). Boogaloo: The Quintessence of American Popular Music. University of Michigan Press. ISBN 0-472-03087-6. pp. 380–381.

Buddah to Casablana Records Hardcover: 310 pages
Publisher: Backbeat (October 6, 2009)

And Party Every Day: The Inside Story Of Casablanca Records Hardcover – November 30, 2009
by Larry Harris (Author), Curt Gooch (Author), Jeff Suhs (Author)

The Nicest Kids in Town: American Bandstand, ...(Paperback) by Matthew F. Delmont
University of California Press (February 22, 2012)

How Blacks Invented Rock and Roll, Ebony Jul 2001
Kevin Chappell

Jet Magazine Pg 37, Feb 14, 1983

George Clinton: Doctor Atomic, The godfather of funk — a musical force for more than five decades — comes clean, by Mark Binelli April 27, 2015

Michigan Music with P.T. Quinn in 2000, http://www.rollingstone.com/music/lists/100-greatest-guitarists-of-all-time-19691231/eddie-hazel-20101202#ixzz430Br9njO
100 Greatest Guitarists: David Fricke's Picks

theguardian.com
Adrian Deevoy,Thursday 23 January 2014)

fastnbulbous.com/Funkadelic: The Afro-Alien Diaspora

(medium.com/cuepoint/From Cocaine Disco to Electronic Dance: the Loaded Legacy of Casablanca Records) Pail Adler, January 29, 2015

References

http://www.nytimes.com/1982/05/09/obituaries/neil-bogart-entertainment-executive-dead-at-39.html"

(2000, P.T. Quinn, George Clinton Speaks, Michigan News)

Remembering The 20 Grand, Detroit's Most Celebrated Nightclub
Comments: 6 Comments | Leave A Comment
Nov 16, 2010 By The Michigan Chronicle

"The Mighty Boosh: The Legend of Old Gregg", TV.com

Eric Olsen, "Tear the Roof Off the Sucker Tonight on PBS with PARLIAMENT FUNKADELIC: One Nation Under a Groove", BC Blogcritics, 11 October 2005. Retrieved 1 January

From Cocaine Disco to Electronic Dance: the Loaded Legacy of Casablanca Records
How an iconic 1970s record label, fueled by substance abuse and bad behavior, survived to embrace a modern generation of dance music

Paul Adler, Cuepoint
Medium's Premier Music Publication: "An ear for the new, a heart for the classics."

Juxtapoz
Pedro Bell "One Nation Under a Dude," Fall 1998
September 17, 2014

WP)By Chris Richards
Washington Post Staff Writer
Monday, April 12, 2010J

1.22.81 Jet. Pg 40
(Page 242) BB)/(Pg 241) BB
Drug Use in the late 70's with Sly Page 232-241-42

(pg 74-75) Cincinnati Magazine

(Pg December 7, 1978; Pg. 23 Jet Magazine

Diem Jones, #1 Bimini Road: Authentic P-Funk Insights, the Motor Booty Affair, Sufi Warrior Publishing, 1996, ISBN 0-9653764-0-0.

Sutherland, Sam (December 9, 1978). "Casablanca's Parliament Push Is Ambitious Multi-Media Campaign". Record World.

Jet 9/14/78,

Jet 6.16.77

Billboard Apr 23, 1977 Pg 44

Ebony 1979, Pg 42

People Magazine , George Clinton Is the Man with the Golden Funk By Robert Windeler; 7.7.1977 Vol 7-No 5

Billboard Magazine Nat Freedland
Billboard Oct 2, 1976

Kempton, Arthur (2005). Boogaloo: The Quintessence of American Popular Music. University of Michigan Press. ISBN 0-472-03087-6. pp. 380–381.

http://fastnbulbous.com/funkadelic-the-afro-alien-diaspora/

Billboard Sep 11, 1971 Ed Ochs Soul Sauce pg 36

Billboard Jun 26, 1971
(P.158, BB)

(Jet 6.3.71) Pg 57

(theguardian.com
Adrian Deevoy, Thursday 23 January 2014)

Billboard Feb 28,1970, Pg 24

George Clinton interviewed by DAVID MILLS:
http://undercoverblackman.blogspot.com/2007/02/q-george-clinton-pt-1.html

33 References

George Clinton on Drugs, Recording With Kendrick and 50 Years of Funk, The P-Funk leader takes us on the mothership in a hilarious new Q&A By Brian Hiatt November 10, 2014. Rolling Stones

George Clinton discusses aliens, conspiracy theories, ERROL NAZARETH
Nov 30, 2004

http://jam.canoe.com/Music/Artists/C/Clinton_George/1997/09/03/743993.html

(www.soulandjazzandfunk.com/interview2428

http://forgottenhits60s.blogspot.com/2013_10_20_archive.html

(soulfuldetroit.com/web16-correctone/08/08 Theresa)

Rolling Stone, George Clinton: Doctor Atomic, The godfather of funk — a musical force for more than five decades — comes clean, By Mark Binelli April 27, 2015

(Andre Hamilton for Allmusic.com)http://solidhitsoul.com/del-larks.html\Mlive.com
Eric Lacy Parliament- Funkadelic's George Clinton to visit Detroit Sound - where it all started

fastnbulbous.com/Funkadelic: The Afro-Alien Diaspora

Billboard Jun 23, 1973 Pg 21

(2000, P.T. Quinn, George Clinton Speaks, Michigan News)

WTOP's Jason Fraley interviews George Clinton November 17th, 2015

The Vermont Review, Interview by Paul Doyle.

George Clinton: Doctor Atomic
The godfather of funk — a musical force for more than five decades — comes clean
By Mark Binelli April 27, 2015

175

United Sound http://detroitsoundconservancy.org/unitedsound/
Detroit Free Press from Detroit, Michigan ·
Page 14
Publication: Detroit Free Press
Location: Detroit, Michigan
Issue Date: Saturday, July 30, 1966

http://www.soul-patrol.com/funk/sidneybarnes.htm

(medium.com/cuepoint/From Cocaine Disco to Electronic Dance: the Loaded Legacy of Casablanca Records) Pail Adler, January 29, 2015

Jet Aug 25, 1966
Chester Higgins

Pigeons & Planes
George Clinton on Kendrick Lamarr: "The Only One I've Seen Do it Like That is Prince"
March 15th, 2016 Pg

Noisey Vice.com
Brian Josephs

THE CONFESSIONS OF RICK JAMES
Memoirs of a Superfreak
By RICK JAMES
ISBN: 9780979097638 / 426 PAGES / $18.95 PAPERBACK

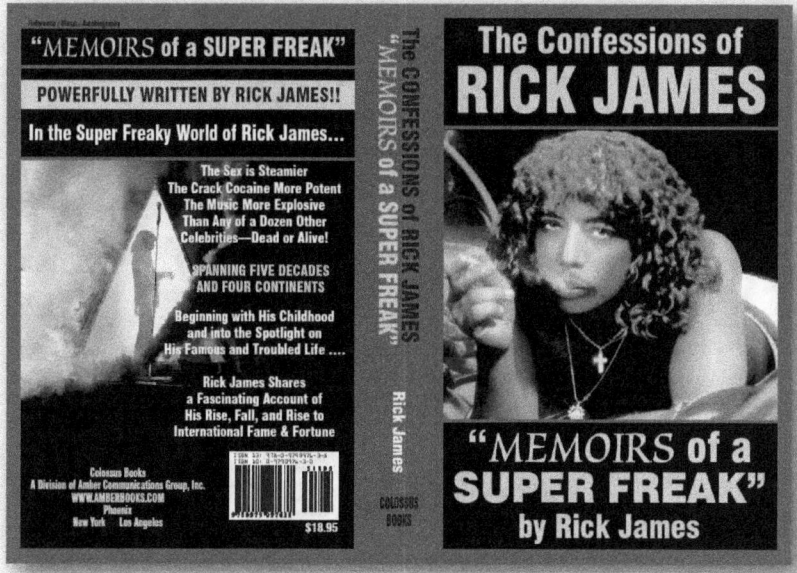

COLOSSUS BOOKS
Available at Amazon.com and Barnes & Noble.com
and wherever books are sold
Email: amberbk@aol.com or Call: 602-743-7211
WWW.TONYROSEENTERPRISES.COM
WWW.AMBERBOOKS.COM

PRINCE IN THE STUDIO (Biography)
By JAKE BROWN
ISBN: 978-0979097669 / 142 PAGES / $16.95 PAPERBACK / $2.99—EBOOK

COLOSSUS BOOKS
Available at Amazon.com, Barnes & Noble.com
and wherever books are sold
Email: amberbk@aol.com or Call: 602-743-7211
WWW.TONYROSEENTERPRISES.COM
WWW.AMBERBOOKS.COM

DR. DRE IN THE STUDIO (Biography)
By JAKE BROWN
ISBN: 9780976773530 / 160 PAGES / $16.95 PAPERBACK / $.99—EBOOK

COLOSSUS BOOKS
Available at Amazon.com, Barnes & Noble.com
and wherever books are sold
Email: amberbk@aol.com or Call: 602-743-7211
WWW.TONYROSEENTERPRISES.COM
WWW.AMBERBOOKS.COM

GOD MADE DIRT (Biography)
By SPENCER SADLER
ISBN: 978-0982492222 / 142 PAGES / $16.95 PAPERBACK / $5.00—EBOOK

COLOSSUS BOOKS
Available at Amazon.com, Barnes & Noble.com
and wherever books are sold
Email: amberbk@aol.com or Call: 602-743-7211
WWW.TONYROSEENTERPRISES.COM
WWW.AMBERBOOKS.COM

ORDER FORM

WWW.AMBERBOOKS.COM

Fax Orders: 480-283-0991 / Telephone Orders: 602-743-7211
Postal Orders: Send Checks & Money Orders Payable to:
   Amber Books
   1334 E. Chandler Blvd., Suite 5-D67, Phoenix, AZ 85048
Online Orders: E-mail: Amberbk@aol.com

____*Beyoncé Before the Legend*, ISBN #: 978-1-937269-42-5, $12.00
____*Kanye West Before the Legend*, ISBN #: 978-1-937269-40-1, $15.00
____*Nicki Minaj: The Woman Who Stole the World*, ISBN #: 978-1-937269-30-2, $12.00
____*Eminem & The Detroit Rap Scene*, ISBN#: 978-1-937269-26-5, $15.00
____*Too Young to Die, Too Old to Live: The Amy Winehouse Story*, ISBN#: 978-1-937269-28-9, $15.00
____*Lady Gaga: Born to Be Free*, ISBN#: 978-1-937269-24-1, $15.00
____*Lil Wayne: An Unauthorized Biography*, ISBN#: 978-0-9824922-3-9, $15.00
____*Black Eyed Peas: Unauthorized Biography*, ISBN#: 978-0-9790976-4-5, $16.95
____*Red Hot Chili Peppers: In the Studio*, ISBN #: 978-0-9790976-5-2, $16.95
____*Dr. Dre In the Studio*, ISBN#: 0-9767735-5-4, $16.95
____*Tupac Shakur—(2Pac) In The Studio*, ISBN#: 0-9767735-0-3, $16.95
____*Jay-Z…and the Roc-A-Fella Dynasty*, ISBN#: 0-9749779-1-8, $16.95
____*Ready to Die: Notorious B.I.G.*, ISBN#: 0-9749779-3-4, $16.95
____*Suge Knight: The Rise, Fall, and Rise of Death Row Records*, ISBN#: 0-9702224-7-5, $21.95
____*50 Cent: No Holds Barred*, ISBN#: 0-9767735-2-X, $16.95
____*Aaliyah—An R&B Princess in Words and Pictures*, ISBN#: 0-9702224-3-2, $10.95
____*You Forgot About Dre: Dr. Dre & Eminem*, ISBN#: 0-9702224-9-1, $10.95
____*Michael Jackson: The King of Pop*, ISBN#: 0-9749779-0-X, $29.95

Name:_____
Company Name:_____
Address:_____
City:_____State:_____Zip:_____
Telephone: (___)_____E-mail:_____

    For Bulk Rates Call: **480-460-1660**   **ORDER NOW**

Beyoncé	$12.00
Kanye West	$15.00
Eminem	$15.00
The Amy Winehouse Story	$15.00
Lady Gaga	$15.00
Nicki Minaj	$12.00
Lil Wayne: An Unauthorized Biography	$15.00
Black Eyed Peas	$16.95
Red Hot Chili Peppers	$16.95
Dr. Dre in the Studio	$16.95
Tupac Shakur	$16.95
Jay-Z…	$16.95
Ready to Die: Notorious B.I.G.	$16.95
Suge Knight:	$21.95
50 Cent: No Holds Barred,	$16.95
Aaliyah—An R&B Princess	$10.95
Dr. Dre & Eminem	$10.95
Michael Jackson: The King of Pop	$29.95

❑ Check ❑ Money Order ❑ Cashiers Check
❑ Credit Card: ❑ MC ❑ Visa ❑ Amex ❑ Discover

CC#_____
Expiration Date:_____
Payable to:
   Amber Books
   1334 E. Chandler Blvd., Suite 5-D67
   Phoenix, AZ 85048

Shipping: $5.00 per book. Allow 7 days for delivery.

Total enclosed: $_____

"SOLID PLATINUM RECORDS AND PRODUCTIONS PRESENTS"
PRINCE CHARLES AND THE CITY BEAT BAND
GREATEST HITS-1979-1984, VOLUME ONE

IN THE STREETS / TIGHT JEANS / YOU ARE MY LOVE / DON'T FAKE THE FUNK /
CASH (CASH MONEY) / CITY LIFE / FISTFUL OF DOLLARS / MORE MONEY /
SKINTIGHT TINA / STONE COLD KILLERS.

ORDER AT
WWW.CDBABY.COM - WWW.ITUNES.COM - WWW.AMAZON.COM
ORDER ORIGINAL PRINCE CHARLES FUNK ALBUMS
GANG WAR - STONE KILLERS - COMBAT ZONE
WWW.AMAZON.COM - WWW.ITUNES.COM - WWW.UNIDISCMUSIC.COM
FOR CD COMPILATION LICENSING - FILM - TELEVISION - SAMPLE LICENSING
CONTACT - TONY ROSE - 602-743-7211 - AMBERBK@AOL.COM
WWW.TONYROSEENTERPRISES.COM

"SOLID PLATINUM RECORDS AND PRODUCTIONS PRESENTS"
PRINCE CHARLES AND THE CITY BEAT BAND
GREATEST DANCE HITS-1981-1987, VOLUME TWO

LOVE IT OR (BEAT THE BUSH) PRINCE CHARLES MIX / BUSH BEAT (INSTRUMENTAL ORIGINAL MIX) / LOVE IT OR (BEAT THE BUSH) DJ SPINNAS RE-FREAKED MIX / JUNGLE STOMP / I'M A FOOL FOR LOVE / I CAN'T STOP LOVING YOU / WE CAN MAKE IT HAPPEN / I'LL BE THERE FOR YOU / VIDEO FREAK (DEFEND IT) TONY ROSE RE-MIX

ORDER AT
WWW.CDBABY.COM - WWW.ITUNES.COM - WWW.AMAZON.COM
ORDER ORIGINAL PRINCE CHARLES FUNK ALBUMS
GANG WAR - STONE KILLERS - COMBAT ZONE
WWW.AMAZON.COM - WWW.ITUNES.COM - WWW.UNIDISCMUSIC.COM
FOR CD COMPILATION LICENSING - FILM - TELEVISION - SAMPLE LICENSING
CONTACT - TONY ROSE - 602-743-7211 - AMBERBK@AOL.COM

AMBER COMMUNICATIONS GROUP, INC.
WWW.TONYROSEENTERPRISES.COM

WWW.TONYROSEENTERPRISES.COM
WWW.AMBERBOOKS.COM
WWW.QUALITYPRESS.INFO
WWW.THEGHETTOBOY.COM
WWW.THEBLACKPOINTOFVIEW.COM

Tony Rose is an NAACP Image Award Winner and the Publisher and CEO of Phoenix, AZ based, Amber Communications Group, Inc., the nation's largest African-American Publisher of Self-Help Books and Music Biographies; The 2013 44th Annual NAACP Image Award Winner for Outstanding Literature; The 2015 First Read Expo Lifetime Achievement Award for Outstanding Literary Work and Leadership; The Los Angeles Leimert Park Book Fair / Jessie Redmon Fauset Book Awards, "2014 African American Book Publisher of the Year"; and The Harlem Book Fair / Phillis Wheatley Book Awards "2013 African American Book Publisher of the Year".

ACGI's imprints include: The NAACP Image Awards winning, Amber Books Publishing; Amber Classics Books - Self-Help Reference Books; Colossus Books - Music Biographies; Amber/Wiley Books - Self Help and Financial Books Co-Published with John Wiley & Sons Inc.; Joyner/Amber Books - Co-Publishing with the Tom Joyner Foundation and Desmoon Books - Fiction.

Tony Rose led the movement towards modern Independent Book Publishing for the African American Self-Publisher and Independent Book Publisher as we know it today.

In 2001 he responded to the needs of the growing market of self-publishers and founded Quality Press, the nation's largest "African American Book Packager For Self-Publishers", in order to accommodate authors who wished to self-publish their books, and placed the Quality Press Self-Publishers Book Division under the direction of Yvonne Rose who is also an Associate Publisher for Amber Communications Group, Inc. and the Director of Quality Press.

Over the last fifteen years Quality Press has been responsible for turning many, many thousands of African American writers into Published Authors and Book Publishers. WWW.QUALITYPRESS.INFO

www.ingramcontent.com/pod-product-compliance
Lightning Source LLC
Chambersburg PA
CBHW071617080526
44588CB00010B/1166